BE
EXCELLENT
on purpose

Sanée Bell

BE EXCELLENT on purpose

Intentional Strategies
for Impactful Leadership

LEAD**FORWARD**

x10

Vision, Experience, Action

Be Excellent on Purpose
© 2019 by Times 10 Publications

These books are available at special discounts when purchased in quantity for premiums, promotions, fundraising, and educational use. For inquiries and details, contact us at WeLeadForward.com.

Published by Times 10
Highland Heights, OH
Times10Books.com

Cover Design by Najdan Mancic
Interior Design by Steven Plummer
Editing by Carrie White-Parrish
Proofreading by Jennifer Jas

Library of Congress Cataloging-in-Publication Data is available.

ISBN: 978-1-948212-15-1
First Printing: July, 2019

This work is dedicated to Marvin, Richmond, and Paige, who inspire and support me to Be Excellent in all that I do.

Table of Contents

Publisher's Foreword

*E*NCOURAGE, EVOLVE, EMPOWER. Mentor, move, motivate. Create, innovate, elevate. Always be listening. Always be learning.

These are the qualities of someone who leads forward. They're not just my words or those of the educators who write leadership books. The words belong to teachers, principals, parents, superintendents, and other education shareholders. Perhaps they are your words, too.

Some time ago, those in my circle—friends, colleagues, and other professionals—discussed ideas around great leadership and the traits of effective leaders. A recurring theme emerged: forward movement. It may have been that moment, during that chat, that "Lead Forward" became more than just words.

Qualities of forward-thinking and forward-moving leaders turned into strategies. Those strategies created experiences and stories. These stories are told by some of education's most dedicated foot soldiers— teacher leaders. Like "be excellent on purpose," a statement Sanée Bell uses often in this book, "teacher leader" is a phrase I use with similar intentionality when discussing the Lead Forward Series.

Lead Forward isn't about just school district leaders or building principals. It's about the journey of teacher leaders doing amazing work in many areas that impact the lives of our children daily. Books in this series are written by people in a variety of roles, including teachers, principals, mentors, and others who possess a unique skill set or idea that can make any Lead Forward reader a better leader, no matter what role they play in education or beyond.

Chrissy Romano Arrabito is a classroom teacher who has a unique understanding of introverted students. She calls them *Quiet Kids*, and in her Lead Forward book, she explains who they are, where they are, and how you can give them a voice.

Jessica Cabeen steered an all-kindergarten building into regional prominence, before taking that experience to a middle school. In *Lead with Grace*, she explains the soft skills of leadership from a unique lens that few possess, but anyone can learn to adopt.

Suzy Brooks and Matthew Joseph bring *Modern Mentor* principles from longtime mentors and mentees. And Sanée Bell shares fascinating stories and powerful strategies that will help you embrace excellence every single day, in this Lead Forward Series flagship book, *Be Excellent on Purpose: Intentional Strategies for Impactful Leadership*.

Stories Strategies Moving Forward

I am proud that part of our mission at Times 10 Publications is to listen to our stakeholders—the people who read our books, listen to our podcasts, engage with our authors on social media, and implement the strategies we share—and give them what they want and what they need. So, we bring you their Stories and Strategies, punctuated by a simple charge at the end of each chapter, called Moving Forward.

Lead Forward Journal

The books in this series are designed to be interactive and we invite you to write on the pages and share your jottings on social media, if you wish. You'll find a Lead Forward Journal section at the end of each chapter, with guided questions and space to write your thoughts and learnings. As a built-in bonus, the journal pages serve as study guides and supplemental tools for book study groups.

Like the Hack Learning Series, the bedrock of Times 10 Books, Lead Forward brings teacher leaders a simple, but powerful, formula for success. Each chapter contains a variety of stories from the authors—part of their continuing journeys to successful leadership in various spaces. Each Story is followed by a Lead Forward Strategy, accompanied by several steps you can use immediately to bring the strategy to your school or classroom. (If you've read a Hack Learning book with its What You Can Do Tomorrow section, you'll recognize the similarity when reading strategies in a Lead Forward book.) At the end of each chapter, you'll find the aforementioned Moving Forward section—a brief summation, along with a takeaway or challenge for you, as you return to leading in your own space.

The Lead Forward Series has been years in the making. Our creative team, along with your input, considered many ideas for what these books should look like to provide the highest value, and invested many hours discussing the topics, authors, chapter format, design, and other facets of this series and our mission. You'll notice that many Lead Forward books have female authors or co-authors. This is by design, as we believe it's important to amplify the voices of women, often underrepresented in education books, in spite of women composing about 70 percent of the jobs in the profession.

The Lead Forward Series helps each of us to be the absolute best we can be. These are our Stories and our Strategies. Yours, mine, and all of the teacher leaders who are doing excellent work to teach and shape our kids and our future. Now, let's Lead Forward.

—MARK BARNES, TEACHER LEADER AND TIMES 10 PUBLICATIONS FOUNDER

Be Excellent on Purpose

"BE EXCELLENT ON **Purpose.**" I don't know many people who wake up each day and say, "I want to be average, below average, or completely ineffective today." In fact, most people intend to have the kind of day that allows them to feel good about their accomplishments and contributions.

That doesn't mean everyone understands what it means to be *excellent*.

So what exactly does it take to be excellent? And how do you do it on purpose? In my mind, to *Be Excellent on Purpose* means following a clear-cut path: being intentional with your time, being intentional with the company you keep, and being intentional about where you focus your thinking and energy. Do those things and you're taking the steps you need to take toward being intentional about being *excellent*.

And the payoff?

Being excellent on purpose means setting a standard for success and doing whatever it takes to close the gap between where you currently are and what you are striving to become. Think about this:

- Would you rather participate in the 100-yard dash ... or win the race?

- Would you rather have a C ... or an A on your report card?

- Would you rather hinder student growth … or inspire them to become the best they can be?

- Would you rather be a leader people want to forget … or one who people would love to work with?

The difference between each set of two choices is nothing more than the amount of effort and energy that goes into making the second option a reality. Excellence is a journey from that first point to the second, where one discovers who they are, what they value, and the principles that drive them. Pursuers of excellence are able to see barriers as obstacles that they can overcome. In fact, it is those barriers and challenges that *strengthen* them in their pursuit of excellence. To *Be Excellent on Purpose* means not making excuses, but making a plan for life and working the plan so it becomes a reality.

Author Will Durant shared great wisdom when he said, "We are what we repeatedly do. Excellence, then, is not an act but a habit." Excellence is not elusive or exclusive. It is not a commodity that can be bought or sold. It is, however, available only to those who want to do the personal work necessary to achieve it. It is a process, a journey that has unexpected stops. But it is the unexpected that prepares us for the next steps.

Let's take those steps together. Let's make excellence a tangible value that you can see in your daily actions.

Have you ever wondered how educators maintain their motivation despite the challenges they face each day? How teachers motivate students who are apathetic about learning? How leaders turn around a school that is underperforming?

The sole premise of *Be Excellent on Purpose* is to show you how to become a leader who can do that—and how to develop habits that will help you lead with excellence. In this book, you will explore the following strategies to help you transform your leadership practice:

Lead lasting change that impacts lives and organizations.

Ensure your school is committed to creating an environment where equity is evident in all practices.

Amplify student voice to design a school that meets the needs of all students.

Define your why and learn how to live your purpose and values.

Frame difficult conversations so the outcomes are productive.

Overcome challenges that hinder teams from being high-performing.

Recognize your impact as a leader, and use your influence to inspire others.

Work with others to create stories worth telling.

Attack your challenges and obstacles.

Reflect and refine your practices.

Dare to be different.

Get ready to break the mold and lead forward into your excellence. Dare to be different by accepting the challenge to *Be Excellent on Purpose!*

Own Your Excellence

If you are going to achieve excellence in big things,
you develop the habit in little matters. Excellence is
not an exception, it is a prevailing attitude.
— COLIN POWELL, U.S. SECRETARY OF
STATE AND FOUR-STAR GENERAL

The Attitude and Actions of Excellence

WHEN I WAS younger, I enjoyed playing outside and competing against the boys. I was fast, athletic, and could hold my own in any competition. Being a kickball standout, the fastest girl at field day, and great at playing football because of my speed and agility were definite assets during recess and when playing in the neighborhood. In the state of Kentucky, basketball is king and we played all year long. When the sound of a basketball hitting the pavement reverberated in the neighborhood, it was a signal that it was time to go outside and play. My neighbors had a basketball goal in their yard and when my mom wouldn't let me go across the street to play at their house, we would play curb ball—an inner-city game of shooting the basketball at a curb instead of through the net. Points are earned when the basketball bounces off the curb into the street.

However you sliced it, I always had a basketball in my hands and was prepared to play the game.

I was also almost always the only female playing, so it was important to show the boys that I belonged. As an NBA fan in the late '80s, I'd already learned to talk smack and play the game with an edgy flair. This came as a result of being a Detroit Pistons fan, and I was especially fond of Isiah Thomas and Bill Laimbeer. I'd watched so many battles between the Pistons and Michael Jordan's Bulls that I developed the ability to sound like a superstar ... even on the days when I wasn't.

The truth was, I had to be better than good, and I had to believe that I was the best, in order to be considered equal competition with the boys. I had to envision myself as an excellent athlete who deserved to be there—and then use that vision to help me improve. This "better than good" belief became the way I approached everything in life. Pushing myself until my good became better and my better became best was how I started facing any challenge. I learned early on in life that if there was an area where I could improve, I needed to do so. I became disinterested in pursuing luck or taking chances on things if I could actually control them instead. If I could influence a situation directly, I looked for a way to do it.

The lesson was this: To achieve excellence, you have to be clear and intentional about what you need to accomplish. Then you have to develop a plan for reaching the goal. You have to build the steps toward becoming excellent.

For me, getting to where I wanted to be started with giving myself a vision of already being there. Developing a personal vision gives us direction. It shows us where we need to go, and helps eliminate distractions.

Knowing where you want to go and visualizing yourself there is a critical step toward pursuing excellence. People tend to underestimate the importance of this intentional planning because it is easier to just dive into the action. But think about it: Without a personal vision, how can a principal lead a school? How can a teacher lead a classroom? How can a superintendent lead a district? It doesn't matter the role you are in; everyone needs to develop a vision of what excellence looks like.

Think of your personal vision as a roadmap, or your internal GPS to where you want to go. See the endpoint, and then lay out the way you'll get there. Then align your daily actions to that personal vision. Once you see the path, it's easier to get to the end without allowing outside influences to distract you.

Knowing where you want to go and visualizing yourself there is a critical step toward pursuing excellence.

If thinking about life in metaphorical terms is helpful, reframe life as a video game. In most video games, the number-one goal is to dodge or defeat the obstacles so that you can win. Things jump out to derail your progress during the game, and if you are not careful, those things will catch you off guard and destroy you. Playing the game without a strategy leaves you vulnerable and open to attacks. Life is the same way. Without a personal vision, you don't have a strategy for success. You have no idea how to traverse the highs and lows of life. Without my vision of being able to compete with the boys in my neighborhood, I quickly would have been dismissed and laughed right off the court. Instead, I envisioned myself belonging, and constructed a reality where I was able to compete with the boys on the court.

Playing basketball in the neighborhood is where I developed the mental and physical toughness to compete, no matter the circumstances. Who knew that the lessons learned on the playground would be so foundational to who I am today? But they taught me one of the most important aspects of life: Establishing a vision is a critical first step to living your excellence.

LEAD**FORWARD**STRATEGY
Create a Personal Vision

- **Think about what you want to achieve in life.** For example, after watching Morgan Freeman in the 1989 film *Lean on Me,* I knew that I wanted to be a principal who was able to take what seemed impossible in the eyes of others and make it possible. Think about what you want to achieve. Be specific. What would your personal vision look like, feel like, and sound like if it became a reality? Write it down in the Lead Forward Journal space at the end of this chapter.

- **Identify the action steps you need to take.** As an assistant principal, I kept a running list of tasks and ideas I wanted to remember to do when I became a principal. Recently, while cleaning files, I came across the notepad and noticed that I'd actually been implementing most of those action items. Although I hadn't seen that list in more than fifteen years, I had spent so much time thinking about and reflecting on the steps, I'd eventually put them into practice without needing the physical list. As you think about your action steps, visualize the outcome you want to achieve. Post your thoughts or create a vision board. This will help you keep your vision at the forefront of your mind. For some, the mind believes what it sees. As you do this visioning work, do not think about possible obstacles. This is not the time to work out personal logistics. Free your mind to just visualize. Do not get caught in the weeds of "what if." You will have time to identify obstacles and challenges later!

- **Develop a plan to eliminate barriers.** Now that you know where you want to go and what you need to do to get there, identify the challenges you must overcome. During this exercise, do not let the words "Yes, but" enter into your plan. It is so easy to find excuses when we are unsure of how to do something new. Do not lump your obstacles into one group. Identify each one individually so that you know exactly what you need to do to address it. Consider the following examples:

  - If you want to pursue an advanced degree, research programs and look for universities with programs that interest you. Think about the style of delivery that best meets your needs. Are you interested in a more traditional face-to-face program, something online, or a blended approach? Answering these questions will help you find the program that will meet your needs—and eliminate barriers ahead of time. If scheduling is a barrier, find ways to manage your calendar so that you are more in control of how you spend your day. If location is a barrier, focus on universities within a certain distance of your home. If cost is a barrier, look for ways to address that ahead of time, through alternative funding sources.

  - Are you struggling to raise a family and be a student? Develop a schedule that will allow you to spend time with your family while working on your degree. It may mean waking up early or staying up late, but you can be a parent and a full-time student. It is not easy, but it is definitely doable. Create a timeline of assignments and projects so that you can work ahead to complete your academic tasks. Be sure that your timeline includes due dates and how much time it will take to complete tasks. This will allow you to add the right amount of work time on the calendar. Organizing this timeline around your family schedule will ensure that you are being purposeful with your time and giving both aspects of your life the focus that they require.

- Are you struggling to implement necessary change in your school or classroom? Identify the needed change, and write down what is preventing the change from happening. Once you identify the obstacle, determine the appropriate action for making the change a reality. For example, is classroom management impacting your ability to teach your students? Think about the routines and procedures in your classroom. If none exist, create them. Record yourself teaching so that you can see yourself in action. Reflect on what you see with a trusted colleague or coach who can give you feedback and tips.

- Do you have a difficult time working with a coworker? Write down your frustrations, as well as your current responses to each frustration. Rethink your responses, which are the only aspects of the relationship you can truly control.

- If you are looking to advance your career, it means finding ways to grow so that you are ready when an opportunity presents itself. I have heard people say that they are not in a place where they can grow. It is not someone else's responsibility to grow you. Your growth belongs to you. Remove those obstacles of stagnation, and bloom where you are planted. Find opportunities to learn and practice new ideas. For example, if you have been studying the leader's role in organizational culture, spend time implementing your learning at your current campus. Reflect on your role in cultivating a school culture that is thriving. What are the specific activities and action steps that create a positive, healthy, and successful culture? Identify the steps you would take to implement this same culture work in a different setting. Although you may be ready to step up your leadership, you won't know how to impact organizational culture on a larger scale if you don't practice those skills on a smaller scale.

When you begin to think about what is stopping you from moving from your current reality to where you want to be, you are uncovering your barriers to success. If achieving your personal vision is important, you will find a way. If it is not, you will find an excuse. The choice is yours. Once you are able to identify the barriers in your life, you can develop a plan to overcome them and move toward excellence.

- **Monitor your progress.** Achieving excellence does not happen instantly or quickly. In James Clear's New York Times bestselling book *Atomic Habits*, he focuses on how the smallest changes can lead to remarkable results. Success is a result of the incremental implementation of actions. Put your action steps on a calendar or task list to make them a priority. In addition, review your progress at the end of the week to monitor how you have used your time. Find accountability partners with whom to share your progress in order to hold yourself accountable. At the end of each week, check in with yourself. Celebrate the high points of your week and make a plan for the areas where you missed the mark. Consider each day a new start. Monitoring your progress will enable you to make short-term adjustments that will ultimately help you accomplish your long-term goal.

It All Goes Back to Your *Why*

Now that you have a personal vision, let's think about your motivation for your goals, and evaluate your "why." Connecting a personal vision to a clearly defined why is the traction you need in order to *Be Excellent on Purpose*. Knowing where you are going will only take you so far. Having a plan is a good first step, but executing the plan with intentionality is when you begin to live out your excellence. Knowing *why* you are doing the work gives you the clearly defined purpose that will help you get to the finish line.

Simon Sinek, author and motivational speaker, discusses the importance of knowing your why in his notable TED Talk, "How Great Leaders Inspire Action." He shares the concept of the golden circle, which includes three concentric circles. The core of the circle represents the why, which is the most fundamental question. The next circle represents how the organization will achieve the why, and the last circle represents what the organization produces. The visual is simple, but the message is powerful.

After watching this talk twice, I began to understand the importance of developing a personal why statement. One would think it would be easy to do, but it took time to flesh it out in my mind. Inspired by Sinek's teachings, I started with the why in the center of the circle, and asked myself the following questions:

- Why do you want to lead?

- What do you hope to accomplish?

- How do your daily actions align with your beliefs?

- What do you want your legacy to be?

Typically, people ask us what we do for a living and we respond with the title of our profession. What if we responded with our why instead of our what? Our why is the purpose we serve—and it immediately makes the what seem a whole lot smaller. For example, I once attended a Bible study where one of the icebreaker questions was what we did during the day. Everyone responded with a job title and the location where they worked. My response was something like this:

> I impact the lives of over 1,200 students, 150 staff members, and my local community by ensuring that the experience each person has each day adds value to their lives, and that they feel safe, supported, and challenged to do their best work. I accomplish this by personally connecting and building capacity in others through active listening and engagement.

By this time, people were so intrigued by my why that they were dying to know what I did each day. I ended by saying, "I am a middle school principal."

Our why gives the what of our life's vision meaning and purpose. This grounding is critical when it comes to ensuring that you are being intentional with your life and that you're leading yourself toward excellence. Take a moment to think about *why* you first entered the education profession. I am sure it had nothing to do with the salary, preparing students for standardized testing, or managing difficult adult behavior. Unfortunately for many educators, over the years, the why becomes suppressed by other issues and tasks. Michael Hyatt, leadership expert, summed it up well when he said, "People lose their way when they lose their why."

To *Be Excellent on Purpose* means ensuring that your daily actions and thoughts are centered on your why. This alignment helps keep your pathways clear toward your goals. Take daily inventory of your actions to make sure you are working within your personal vision. The only way to make your vision a reality is to connect it to your why.

LEAD**FORWARD**STRATEGY
Develop Your Why (and How and What)

- **Start from within and reflect on why you do what you do.** Dig deep and be honest with yourself, then write down your thoughts. These are your private thoughts, so don't try to suppress them or force them to fit someone else's expectations. Fabricating your responses or trying to make them sound good is inauthentic. Think about your responses as your manifesto. Are your actions reflective of your personal vision? How are you living your excellence each day? If those who know you best could read your thoughts, would they say that the words definitely reflect who you are on a daily basis?

  On the other hand, do not be alarmed if what you write differs from what you currently project to others. Sometimes we lose sight of our why, or we may be in a position that does not allow us to live out our why. No matter where you end up, remember that it is also possible that your motivation has shifted. If you have had the same position for quite some time, you might have outgrown it—even if it used to be your ultimate goal. You may discover that your growth is in another place.

Perhaps it is time for you to pursue other interests that will challenge you to grow. Why settle for good when excellent is within your reach?

No matter what you discover during this reflection, stick with the process. This will take time, so be patient. Discovering and developing your why is the foundation for living your excellence in a way that will help you lead forward. As you engage in this work, consider the following questions:

- Why do I engage in my current work?

- What excites me about my personal and professional goals?

- What is my greatest hope for myself?

- What passions drive me in relation to my purpose?

- What is my motivation for living out my why?

Here is an example of a why statement:

"To help students and educators unleash their inner power so they can create a life where they feel successful, inspired, and fulfilled."

- **Identify your how.** After fleshing out the why, you are ready to explore *how* you are going to accomplish your why. Developing the how gives your why life. Think about your how as a set of values that can be seen in your daily interactions with others, and which will help you achieve your why. These are, in effect, the tools you will use to achieve excellence. These core values are broad themes through which you can filter all of your actions. Integrity, excellence, teamwork, and service are examples of core values. When reflecting on your how, be specific about how your values will help you to live your why every day.

- If you are struggling to think of words that capture your core values, visit the websites of James Clear and Brené Brown, and search for their lists of core values. Seeing a list of values may help to jog your brain. For example, one of my core values is authenticity. It is important to me that I work with others who are honest and truthful. When I feel that I am working in a setting that is outside of this core value, I find it difficult to engage with others. Achievement is another example of a value that is important to me. Being able to set a goal and accomplish it gives me satisfaction and fulfillment. When you engage in this exercise, if you keep circling back to the same words, those are probably the values from which you are working.

- As you review the words, select the ones that best reflect who you are as a person. Then move on to brainstorming about specific actions and thoughts that reflect those values. For example, in order to create an environment where authenticity is valued on my team, I need to create an environment where everyone feels safe and supported to do their best work. In order to do this, it is important that we get to know each other as individuals. If recognition is a value, think about how you can create opportunities to recognize others for their work. The power of discovering your values and the values of those you work with is that it gives you the opportunity to create an environment designed to meet the needs of each person on your team—and help you all work toward excellence.

Here is an example of a how statement:

"Working every day to create an environment of acceptance, respect, and recognition."

- **Ensure that your what reflects your why.** Your *what* is the vehicle and context for how you will accomplish your why. Simon Sinek said, "What you do serves as the proof of what you believe." What we choose to do or not do shows others our priorities. Be certain that your daily actions and interactions clearly demonstrate your why. When you are working outside of your why, it means you have lost focus on what you should be doing. Write your own why-how-what statement using the following template from Sinek:

  I (Why Statement). I do this by (How Statement). Being a (What Statement) is how I live my why daily.

  Here is an example of a why-how-what statement:

  "I help students and educators unleash their inner power so that they can create a life where they feel successful, inspired, and fulfilled. I do this by working every day to create an environment of acceptance, respect, and recognition. Being a Teacher Leader is how I live my why daily."

When you evaluate your why, you are able to elevate your purpose. Being able to articulate why you do what you do gives your purpose depth and meaning, and when you have a clearly defined purpose, you are equipped to handle the potential threats and challenges you may encounter along the way. When you know your why, the pathway to excellence is clear.

Vulnerability Builds Strength

Have you ever seen a person who is so determined to accomplish their goals that nothing can stand in their way? Those who are driven by their why may put themselves in a position that others would not dare to try. My path to the elementary principal seat was not a traditional one. Because all of my teaching and administrative experience was at the secondary level, becoming an elementary principal meant that I made myself more vulnerable than I had ever been in my career, and it was frightening.

After six years as an assistant principal, this was not only going to be my first principalship, but also my first time being in an elementary school since I was a fifth-grade student. I knew nothing about what happened in an elementary school, and this not knowing was the reason I had never applied for an elementary principalship before.

I had limited knowledge about the elementary experience, including the day-to-day logistics, the systems and structures, and the curriculum. My lack of knowledge was initially extremely challenging. But I did have a strategy for success, which included asking for help. At the beginning of my new role, I empowered those around me by sharing my limitations and strengths with my staff. "This is a new learning experience for me, and your help will definitely be needed."

Being transparent about where I needed help and asking more questions than I gave answers actually helped me to grow into a better leader. I made myself vulnerable, and it allowed me to create an environment where we shared leadership. It gave me the opportunity to share power *with* people instead of holding power *over* people. It also allowed me to learn from multiple sources, which broadened my knowledge and skills.

Being able to say, "I don't know but I am willing to learn" takes vulnerability, but it gives a leader the chance to learn, grow, and evolve into an even better leader. Practicing vulnerability takes courage, strength, and resolve—but it will lead to excellence.

If you want to make excellence your purpose and grow toward your ultimate vision of yourself, you must make vulnerability part of your leadership practice. Being willing to embrace vulnerability opens you up to a world of ideas and possibilities that you didn't know existed. We will never know how to do everything; however, we do need to know how to recognize when to ask others for help. Practicing vulnerability means being comfortable with self-improvement and growth. When we are learning, we are evolving into a better version of ourselves and taking steps toward being excellent on purpose. The fear of looking incompetent or like we don't have it all together often stops us from admitting when we don't know how to do something, or that we need help. I want to challenge that thinking. Acting as if we have it all together when we know we don't means we are not being honest with ourselves and authentic with others. Acknowledge when you need help. Ask for what you need and be willing to let others help you.

LEAD**FORWARD**STRATEGY
Practice Vulnerability

- **Understand that people respect honesty.** More important, be honest with yourself about where you may need additional support. By recognizing where you need help and then identifying people and resources that can assist you in your growth, you are practicing vulnerability responsibly.

- **Seek to become familiar with the unknown.** When is the last time you did something that absolutely scared you? Do something that makes you feel uncomfortable, not because it is against your values or beliefs, but because you have no idea how to do it. Challenge yourself to get comfortable with being uncomfortable. It is easy to stay in the safe zone. Push yourself out of the realm of comfort by researching and implementing a new tool or strategy, forming a new habit, or talking with others who challenge you philosophically. Be sure to put strategies in place that will help you rise to the challenge. Approach the challenge with your eyes and ears wide open, and use the growth to lead you toward the excellence you envision for yourself.

- **Journal your journey.** Discover the value of recording your thoughts and feelings when you are navigating uncharted waters. Being able to look back at where you started in relation to where you are today gives you the opportunity to examine how you have grown as a leader. Journaling also helps you explore and check your emotions, gives you the chance to practice transparency, and allows you to reflect on the journey. Write down your daily wins. What worked well for you today? Make note of why those were wins. Identify the action steps that led to your success. In addition, think about where you missed the mark. What caused your lack of progress? How will you make the necessary adjustments moving forward? Journaling is an outlet where you can be your most vulnerable self. That is, of course, if you believe in being honest and transparent with your thoughts and feelings. Before you can be vulnerable with others, you must practice being vulnerable with yourself.

MOVING**FORWARD**

To live a life of excellence, engage in the work of developing yourself. Every experience we encounter is a setup for something else. In 2016, Brené Brown interviewed me for an online course she was developing for educators. Brown is a research professor at the University of Houston, and she is one of my favorite authors and speakers. She has written books about leadership, courage, shame, vulnerability, and empathy, and her TED Talk, "The Power of Vulnerability," has been viewed over 36 million times. Participating with her in this experience helped me realize why I downplay the significance of my accomplishments and shy away from compliments.

As a somewhat introverted person, I'm uncomfortable being the center of attention, so it was a bit unsettling when I was named Elementary Principal of the Year. When I shared this experience with Brown and described my inability to fully enjoy the accomplishment, she helped me to see that I was my own worst critic. I was forbidding myself to feel joy, and this decision caused me to miss out on one of the most joyous moments of my career. Instead of enjoying what I had earned because of my intentionality, hard work, and work ethic, I focused on the possibility that others would think that I was not worthy of the recognition. Unfortunately, being our own worst critic can prevent us from celebrating our accomplishments. We all know students and educators who shy away from recognition. For expert guidance on helping them to shine in their own ways, see *Quiet Kids Count*, a Lead Forward Series book about introverts by an introvert, Chrissy Romano Arrabito.

It wasn't until author Jimmy Casas told me, "Don't ever let anyone take away your excellence," that I realized I was the "anyone" he was referring to. There will always be other critics in the arena who criticize what we do or achieve, but we must realize that we can't be one of them. We earned our excellence by developing our vision, living our why, and being willing to put ourselves out there despite the risk—so own it!

When we are striving to *Be Excellent on Purpose*, we must expect success to be the result. We must dare to be different, not so we can stand out from the crowd for the purposes of elevating ourselves or our accomplishments, but so we can stand up for the students and teachers we serve each day. Seeking to be better than good and working so that our better becomes best means that our profession and our students win. Practicing vulnerability doesn't mean practicing shame. It just means recognizing that the accolades we receive on our journey are results of the seeds we have planted and cultivated along the way.

By planting seeds of excellence, you have taken the time to till the ground and get it ready so that the seeds can take root and thrive. There are no paved paths to excellence, but if you pursue it and your passion fuels it, your seeds will grow. To *Be Excellent on Purpose* begins by knowing who you are, where you are going, and what you stand for. It is not a step-by-step program, but it does include the self-work that leads to excellence. Be humble, but be proud of the person you are becoming. You are being intentional with your life, so you should expect, accept, and celebrate the results.

CHAPTER 1
LEAD**FORWARD**JOURNAL

My personal vision

I want to achieve ...

_____

_____

_____

A few steps I'll take ...

_____

_____

_____

Barriers I may encounter ...

_____

_____

_____

Developing my WHY

How am I living my excellence each day?

_____

_____

_____

What values contribute to living my excellence?

_____

_____

_____

Seeking and receiving help

Who or what should I seek help from in developing my personal vision?

_____

_____

_____

_____

_____

What aspects of my vision frighten me?

_____

_____

_____

_____

How will I overcome these fears?

_____

_____

_____

_____

_____

Share your journal entries and ideas at #LeadForward on Twitter.

CHAPTER 2

Understand the Power of Words and Actions

*Our words can either inspire greatness, or they can
extinguish the potential of those they lead.*
— TANVEER NASEER, SPEAKER AND LEADERSHIP EXPERT

HEN YOU ARE sitting in front of an interview committee, the only thing you are thinking about is leaving a lasting impression on the people around the table. One year, while I was interviewing with a panel of teachers, parents, and district personnel discussing my leadership experience and what I would bring to their school, they asked if I had any final words before the conversation came to an end. I remember saying that I would lead with purpose, intention, and excellence. As a school, we would *Be Excellent on Purpose*, which meant we would strive for excellence in all we did. The heads began to nod, eyebrows rose, wide smiles appeared, and my boss responded by repeating the phrase and saying, "That is how to close an interview!"

On that day, this personal motto became a public proclamation of my leadership, and the motto of our school. Every year, in organizations all over the world, teams develop themes, taglines, and brands to guide their work for the year. They order T-shirts, pens, banners, and other swag items with the theme branded on them. They even change the business letterhead and email signature to reflect the organization's theme. When possible, the theme is incorporated into every speech that leaders share. Don't get me wrong; there is nothing wrong with this. As a principal, I have developed many yearly themes throughout my career. I have several shirts with cool theme graphics plastered all over them. In fact, I have a quilt that was made with many of the theme T-shirts from over the years.

The phrase *Be Excellent on Purpose* was not born as a theme. I began using it personally as a quick way of saying that success is a result of intentional planning and hard work. The essence of the phrase resembles something I probably said on the basketball court years ago. Some athletes have the ability to make their craft look effortless and easy. However, we know that the athleticism and outstanding play we enjoy watching does not happen by chance. So much of it is about the work they put in behind the scenes.

Reaching peak performance is the same for everyone—a result of intentional focus and action. *Be Excellent on Purpose* means being intentional in all aspects of the day. This realization and its adoption into my own life created a theme. As leaders, we must model our words to promote our vision and encourage others to join us.

We frame the journey for those we lead. From the moment we step in front of our staff, department, or classroom, we are on. They are looking to us for guidance, direction, and validation. We must also recognize that our influence can impact the organization and the people working in it both positively and negatively. It's our job to make sure that we have a positive impact. The organizations we lead are molded by our words, actions, and inactions. Everything we do as a leader matters—everything. And whether you are aware of it or not, everyone is watching. As popular education author and presenter Todd Whitaker says, "When the principal sneezes, the whole school catches a cold."

Every organization has a story, and in most cases, the story is developed as a result of its leadership. Think about the typical classroom. Most classrooms are a reflection of the teacher's personality and priorities, just as a school is usually a reflection of the leadership. As you reflect on the story of your classroom or school, think about whether your space reflects who you are as a person and what you believe about the success of students or staff. Is your school or classroom an environment people are running away from … or running toward? Your leadership defines the organization. Be sure that you are framing the organization for excellence.

People want to identify with leaders who excite and energize them to do more collectively than they are able to achieve individually.

LEAD**FORWARD**STRATEGY
Define Your Organization

- **Conduct a personality check.** Your school or classroom culture is a direct reflection of your leadership. Do you like what you see? When you work with others to define what your organization is about, be sure to determine whether the words you speak truly reflect the environment you're building. For example, if "Learning for All" is the motto of the school, look around and decide whether each individual student shows progress and achievement at their highest level. Better yet, do the actions of the adults and the systems and structures ensure that all students are thriving? Are the words you're using actually translating into actions, or are they just words?

In order to determine whether the words reflect daily actions, observe and record what you see happening and ask questions to gain a better understanding. If you see something you don't like or something that goes against your school's themes or your plans for the school, it is your responsibility to change it. Focus on what you can control and solicit help from others to assist you in making the change. Culture work belongs to the group, but the leader is responsible for leading the way. Establish and share your vision so that the organization becomes a reflection of who you are and what you are working to accomplish as a leader.

- **Clearly articulate and share the vision.** When it comes to leadership, establishing your vision for yourself isn't enough. You must establish and communicate a clear vision for the entire organization to motivate and inspire others. People want to identify with leaders who excite and energize them to do more collectively than they are able to achieve individually. When establishing a vision, consider the following questions:

  - Have you communicated your vision to the point that it inspires others?

  - Is your vision visible in your school? Classroom? District?

  - What evidence do you have that your vision is motivating and inspiring to others?

  - Do your daily interactions and the actions of your staff reflect the vision?

  Remember, a vision is what you are working to build with your words. Be sure that the words you speak match your actions. A foundational principle to being excellent on purpose is intentionality. Do not leave anything to chance.

- **Challenge the status quo.** Find the average within your organization and work with your team to identify strategies and resources that can move the average to the next level. Use multiple sources of data, both quantitative and qualitative, to identify where to begin those improvement efforts. What you say and how you say it will determine how successful you'll be in this regard. Some leaders can kill the challenge before it is given, while others finesse their words to encourage and inspire people to change. Challenging the status quo does not mean criticizing the work that has occurred. It does not mean that what is currently happening is wrong or ineffective. It just means that in order to move something that is good toward being excellent, we must commit to continuous improvement. The following phrases may be helpful to start the conversation:

  - Where can we continue to grow and improve?

  - Is this method or strategy the only way to achieve our goal?

  - How are other organizations addressing this issue?

  - Are we satisfied with our current results? If not, what do we need to do to move us forward? If so, are the results the best they can be?

As a leader, your job is to call out areas where underperformance and mediocrity exist, not in a way that demeans or diminishes, but in a way that inspires and

motivates. Mediocrity and underperformance cannot
thrive in an organization that is committed to excellence.

Focus on What's Strong Instead of What's Wrong

Once you have communicated the vision for your campus, it is time
to start measuring the impact of the words and actions on the work
being done. After becoming the principal at my current campus,
I wanted to make sure that the phrase *Be Excellent on Purpose*
became more than just words. For words to become actions, they
must not only be spoken, but modeled.

After the school year got underway, we provided our entire student body with T-shirts with the phrase *Be Excellent on Purpose*
printed on them. Prior to passing them out, we discussed the
power of those words and what it meant to live by them in our
school and personal lives. Staff members began using the phrase
to frame their talks with students and colleagues. Students then
began using the words with each other. Being consistent with the
message and the meaning helped move the words from something
catchy and fun to say, to an anchor of what our school was about
and how we would achieve excellence. Once the staff and students
began to take ownership of our motto, they started to unite around
that common purpose.

For example, while conducting a formal observation, I overheard
a conversation between two students. Moving swiftly between the
students in passing as they tended to their normal routines, I heard
one student say, "Dr. Bell is coming today, so we definitely have to
be excellent on purpose." Her classmate grinned and nodded her
head in my direction. The student slowly turned around, her eyes
meeting mine, and we both chuckled. She gave me a hug as we
greeted one another, and without any explanation, we both knew
what she meant by the comment.

For our students, staff, and community, *Be Excellent on Purpose* was about becoming a better student, educator, school, and community through intentional actions and purposeful engagement. We measured every decision and action against the barometer of excellence that we established as a staff while conducting our organization's personality assessment. Where we fell short, we put actions into place to overcome those obstacles. Striving for excellence always trumped making excuses. As this phrase began to saturate our setting, our staff conversations changed from talks where we focused on finding excuses to talks where we focused on finding solutions.

When we pursue excellence, excuses are not invited to the conversation.

Focusing on solutions means changing the way we look at things, in both word and deed. In our school, that started with the pursuit of excellence and it grew to empowering everyone to innovate and seek new ways to solve problems. We all began challenging each other to evaluate the effectiveness of our practices. Were we really being excellent on purpose, or were we resting on our laurels? Just because something had always been done doesn't mean that it had been done well. Working together toward a common purpose through shared decision-making—and a shared goal—created voice and ownership within the organization. This kept the organization focused on what was going well, which motivated individuals to find solutions to address areas that could be better.

By focusing on what's strong instead of what's wrong, we see our organizations as thriving and evolving. Through this lens, we can come up with solutions that will make us even better because we are working from a strengths-based angle. Think about it. If you are seeing progress in most areas, and use that as a measure, it will make it easier to spot the areas where you're *not* seeing progress. The next natural step is to figure out how to make those not-so-great areas better. If you're working from a deficit mindset instead, all you focus on are the insurmountable tasks viewed through a negative lens.

When communicating progress, reframe how you share the progress with your staff. Conduct success reviews where you highlight areas of growth and progress toward goals. Communicate what is working so that your team feels encouraged by the progress they're making. This will help increase the collective optimism of the group, which will generate the positive energy your organization needs to continue moving forward.

LEAD**FORWARD**STRATEGY
Find the Diamonds

- **Identify an area of focus**. When you're looking at a whole school system, structure, or initiative with a leadership team, identify one gem of an area on which to focus the team's thinking. Identify what is working and why it is successful. This will give the team time to generate positive energy around the benefits of the focus area. Drilling down to the effectiveness is hard to do when it is not the intentional focus. Next, identify what is not working quite so well, and create strategies to fix the ineffective areas. Be sure to focus on specific barriers and obstacles that are not working, rather than on people. Record the thoughts on chart paper so that everyone can add to, agree with, or even disagree with what others share. This gives each individual the opportunity to have their voice heard, and also strengthens the conversation around the most important collective thoughts of the team.

Find the Diamonds Processing Tool

Focus Area:

What Is Working?	What Is Not Working?

Solution Summary:

- **Own the work.** When working with a leadership team, a professional learning community, or any group charged with leading an initiative, encourage them to follow through on your leadership lessons and own the work they are charged with leading. For example, if a school is implementing a new learning strategy school-wide, initiate checks throughout the school year to determine the impact of the strategy on learning. If the group reviews student work and determines that there has been no change in student learning, ask them to determine the next steps. It would be easy to blame the lack of growth on others, especially the students, but an effective leadership team focuses on what they can control and comes up with solutions and strategies to move the initiative forward. This is where responsibility and accountability begin to create ownership among the group, and it spends more energy on solutions instead of excuses. Remember that we are looking for ways to *Be Excellent on Purpose*—and that means constantly moving forward through word and deed to help the end result shine, rather than getting stuck on something that doesn't seem to be working.

- **Develop potential solutions and identify potential pitfalls.** As a team, commit to turning a solution idea into a reality by creating a team mission statement and being transparent about who will take the lead on key action items. It's key to communicate and dedicate yourselves to the power of words! Once you've committed, as a team, continue to check back in to track progress. Make sure, too, that your actions in support of the solutions match the team mission statement. As you develop solutions, identify potential challenges and pushback that could derail your progress. Be prepared to counter those claims with a well-thought-out plan. Remember, everything new is hard until it becomes easy. The role of the leader is to encourage the team to keep moving forward by keeping the group focused on the goal.

The Power of the Locker Room Speech

When organizations approach a challenge or setback, the words and actions of the leader are significant factors in how well the organization is able to recover and move forward. There is no better illustration of this than the power of a coach who is addressing his team during moments of triumph or despair in the locker room. In

2016, ESPN recorded a short vignette of some of the most powerful college football locker room speeches. One of the speeches was by Syracuse football coach Dino Babers, who delivered a powerful speech after his team upset Virginia Tech. This was a signature win for the Syracuse program since they had not beaten a top twenty-five team since 2001. If you haven't seen one of Coach Babers' victory speeches, I strongly encourage you to watch one. I guarantee that you will be motivated to get up and take action.

Coach Babers does the following in every speech:

- Focuses on the mission of the program.

- Points out the obstacle that the team overcame.

- Celebrates the achievement and effort of the group.

- Identifies the next challenge ahead.

- Uses his words and emotions to inspire the group.

- Speaks from the heart.

All of the coaches that ESPN showcased were full of passion, which allowed their speeches to become more than just words, but Coach Babers made me believe that I could suit up and play for the Orangemen! His words and visible emotions moved the group to believe in more than just their individual talent and the talent of their teammates. He made the team believe they were unbeatable on the field and in life—and believing is half the battle.

Prior achievement builds confidence in teams and groups. In sports, when an underdog team wins, the group belief rises exponentially and they start to believe in the possible more than the impossible. If a group has not been able to achieve success, it is helpful for them to see groups with similar circumstances and challenges achieving success. When they see that it has been done before by people in similar situations, they believe they can replicate the same success. Every organization needs a starting point and something to believe in.

In some situations, the leader has to believe more than the team to get them to the starting point—and the leader must be vocal about it. It is a leader's responsibility to lead with strong belief and conviction, even if the leader is unsure how the task will get done. Think about popular movies based on students or teachers overcoming obstacles: *Freedom Writers*, *The Great Debaters*, *Stand and Deliver*, and *Lean on Me*, to name just a few. The students and teachers portrayed in these movies faced significant challenges and circumstances that were true barriers and obstacles to learning and success. In each of those movies and countless others like them, something in the leader caused those they were leading to believe they could achieve something they never believed was possible. Although the belief was not there initially, through intentional actions and inspiring words from the leader, they were able to achieve unimaginable success together.

During my first year of coaching basketball, the program was horrible and did not have a tradition of winning. I later learned that no one else was even interested in coaching the team, which is why I was the lucky winner when I was hired. After the first practice, I understood why. Although there was some individual talent on the team, it was not enough to be competitive, plus most of the players had less-than-stellar attitudes and poor work ethics. Knowledge of the game was pretty limited. This team went into every game expecting to lose; however, it was important to will my team into believing otherwise.

Learning how to help people grow and improve takes time. I started by finding something to celebrate after each loss. Each time I did so, the team started to see where they were growing and improving. We didn't win our first game until the last game of the season, and when we did, you would have thought it was a championship victory. That win propelled us into success the following year. The team had to experience a glimpse of success in order to get hungry for more.

On top of that, I altered my own path in order to better lead the team. Instead of sticking with my original game plan, I adjusted my coaching style to focus on the strengths of my players. I unlearned and relearned how to best coach my athletes. Being able to scrap my game plan to learn something new helped me grow as a coach, and I came up with an important new motto: When working to grow and develop others, recognize their strengths and build on them. Of course, it is also important to recognize limitations, and not make foolish leadership moves without the personnel to execute the plan.

Most important, realize that making adjustments to your plan doesn't mean lowering your expectations. It means increasing your level of support to help the group be successful. It means changing both actions and mindsets. We all have to start somewhere. It is acceptable to be where you currently are in your growth process, but it is unacceptable to stay there.

Use your words to build the collective efficacy of the group. Words breathe life into individuals and organizations. When people can't believe in themselves or the mission of the group, the words of a leader can propel them to action and fuel their fire. Words, when said in the right way, can alter someone's beliefs and change their mind. A simple choice of words can be the difference in someone accepting and believing your words to be true. When a leader understands that what they say and how they say it can inspire, motivate, and energize a group, they are more intentional about the way they use their words.

LEAD**FORWARD**STRATEGY
Develop Champions

- **Unite the group**. Bring your group together by finding the common purpose and mission, and communicate these words in a passionate way. Passion is what fuels us when we are faced with challenges. It drives us to reach specific goals despite the obstacles in the way. Passion is not an emotion that we can manufacture; however, a leader who exudes passion can will their team to success. Be clear about communicating the purpose of a group, identifying the outcome the group is striving to achieve, and sharing how the group will reach the goal. For example, review the group goals periodically throughout the year. If the only time the goals are reviewed is when they are written and again at the end of the year, the group will fail at making any significant progress. Together, look at goals monthly or quarterly and be vocal about what's going well and where to improve. Identify and assign specific actions and steps so that everyone has a clear path to success.

- **Recognize the efforts of individuals.** In all group successes, there are key individuals who do extraordinary things to make the group better. Recognize these efforts, not just to single out individual contributions, but to highlight the types of contributions that are critical to group success. This provides a model for others to follow. It also shows the group that they need and value each team member's individual contribution. One way to recognize individuals is by writing a note expressing gratitude. Handwritten notes are powerful because most communication comes to us electronically. A simple note of recognition goes a long way. Taking the time to recognize someone face to face is another effective strategy. Let people know how they impact you personally and how their efforts make the organization better. Positive reinforcement from a leader has a great return on the investment of your time, and those words make the entire group stronger.

MOVING**FORWARD**

Your words can unite people. They can let everyone know they are part of something greater collectively than they would be individually. Belief in the group and what it is trying to accomplish is a key component of organizational success. As the leader, it is your responsibility to raise the awareness and interest of the group around the mission. It's your job to help them look beyond themselves for the good of the group.

Although a leader is in a position to create goals and a vision for a group, the leader can't do the work alone. It takes everyone working together, collectively, to achieve excellence. When people believe they can do something, they see setbacks as nothing more than temporary obstacles. The stronger the belief in the group, the more focused and committed the group will be in working together to achieve the goal. They understand that each person is critical to the success of the group, and this belief influences what people choose to do as a group and the amount of effort they exert. Words used to uplift, inspire, and motivate can leave a lasting legacy within the organization and the individuals connected to it. Words matter; choose them wisely.

CHAPTER 2
LEAD**FORWARD**JOURNAL

Define your organization

I will frame my organization for excellence by ...

_____

_____

_____

Ways that I will communicate the vision include ...

_____

_____

_____

Find the diamonds

Identify three areas where my organization is thriving:

_____

_____

_____

What are the contributing factors to my current success in each area?

_____

_____

_____

Select one area in my organization where I want to improve.

_____

_____

_____

_____

Improvement focus

How can I use the success identified in other areas to help me develop a plan to achieve success in a problem area?

_____

_____

_____

_____

List the barriers that are preventing me from reaching the desired outcome.

_____

_____

_____

_____

The following people can help move the organization forward because of the strengths they possess:

Change agent 1:

Strengths:

Change agent 2:

Strengths:

Change agent 3:

Strengths:

Share your journal entries and ideas at #LeadForward on Twitter.

CHAPTER 3
Expand Your Connections

You are the average of the five people you spend the most time with.
— JIM ROHN, ENTREPRENEUR, AUTHOR, AND SPEAKER

Wireless Relationships

ACCORDING TO A *Big Think* blog post, inventor Nikola Tesla made the following statement in a 1926 interview conducted by John B. Kennedy:

"When wireless is perfectly applied the whole earth will be converted into a huge brain, which in fact it is, all things being particles of a real and rhythmic whole. We shall be able to communicate with one another instantly, irrespective of distance. Not only this, but through television and telephony we shall see and hear one another as perfectly as though we were face to face, despite intervening distances of thousands of miles; and the instruments through which we shall be able to do this will be amazingly simple compared with our present telephone. A man will be able to carry one in his vest pocket."[1]

This statement certainly represents our current world, and I am sure we can all agree that our world transformed when devices got smarter. Along with smartphones came new ways of engaging with smarter people from all over the world. And those ways of engaging changed everything in education and in life itself. Today, it's impossible to try to imagine a world without those tools, which help me connect with educators around the globe. What the world will look like twenty-five years from now is even more difficult to foresee. I can't help but wonder what Tesla would say today about our future.

It's important to realize that while the devices have become a way of life, the devices themselves do not fuel us. It is what we are able to do with them that keeps them attached to us. During the initial phases of the telephone, the only function was to communicate. Our smartphones have transformed the ways we communicate, create, collaborate, and connect with others. For example, while creating this book, 95 percent of the communication took place through smartphones. Our smartphones have allowed us to expand our connections to include people we might not meet face to face, in places we may never visit in person. I have connected with and learned from individuals who live around the world, and I'm sure you have too.

That opportunity to grow and learn from people in distant lands is available to all of us through current technology. Those who are striving to *Be Excellent on Purpose* will seize that opportunity by capitalizing on this ability to connect, learn, and grow.

The quickest and easiest way to head out on this journey is through social media, which gives us access to more people and more knowledge. Keeping up with friends and family is great, but what about all the opportunities for learning? And beyond that, what about the opportunities to grow and push beyond our current realities? They are virtually limitless in this realm!

Professionally, social media has changed my world. Being connected with others has given me the opportunity to explore possibilities that

I previously didn't know were available, and I'm able to use social media to expand as a leader. I have broadened my network to include leaders from different industries across the world, and I invest time in learning from them. Connecting with others gives you the opportunity to redefine your excellence by taking what others teach you and using it in your own life. Just as Nikola Tesla predicted, we are able to learn more because we have a tool that allows us to access and explore the thoughts of so many others. But it only works if you *use* it.

LEAD**FORWARD**STRATEGY
Get Connected

- **Build a personal and professional network.** Think about the sources you're currently using for personal and professional growth. If you can't identify any sources, or you feel that the sources you have are lacking, that is where you need to begin your work. A whole world extends beyond your current sources. Other educators in our fields have already tackled some of our most pressing challenges. Why suffer alone when others are out there willing to help you on your journey? Write down areas where you want to learn and grow, and this will help you to identify the types of people you need to connect with.

  Be intentional with your connections, so that each one addresses your immediate needs. For example, if I have aspirations to move into a central office role in the future, then I need to expand my connections to include people who serve in those roles. This will give me the opportunity to learn about the transition and give me a glimpse into what the role could look like. As you build your connections, you will find that your knowledge base begins to expand. Being connected with others also exposes you to opportunities that may not have been available to you otherwise.

- **Explore and use tools that meet your needs.** When I first began using social media for professional growth, I was completely overwhelmed. It took some time before I understood how these simple tools could impact my growth as a professional. Start with where you are comfortable, but start somewhere. Although the tools are ever changing, social networking communities for educators exist on various platforms.

  We Are Teachers, an organization dedicated to inspiring and supporting educators, has created several Facebook groups and pages geared toward idea-sharing and relationship-building with other educators. Facebook groups are a great way to connect with other educators who are passionate about a topic or want to learn more about a particular area. You can search for topics to see what groups are available. For example, if you are interested in standards-based grading, Teachers Throwing Out Grades and Standards Based Learning and Grading are two active Facebook communities that frequently share resources and ideas on this topic. I invite you to join the Lead Forward Series group on Facebook for ideas, connections, and resources for educators. (See the Resources from Times 10 section in the back of this book.)

  Twitter is another popular social networking tool. In the article "Why Teachers Are Turning to Twitter," author Brendon Hyndman, educational researcher and course director of postgraduate studies in education at Charles Sturt University, talks about teachers needing better support, resources, and relationships if they want to prevent isolation. Twitter offers educators a simple platform where they can connect. Use it to self-direct your professional growth and develop connections that extend beyond the platform. If you are new to Twitter, check out the article "Twitter for Teachers" on Kathy Schrock's Guide to Everything website for a comprehensive list of tips and resources. Growing your network can lead you to tools that increase your learning and productivity.

When we get serious about who we are engaging with personally and professionally, we are not only committing to being excellent for ourselves, but we are committing to being excellent for those who are counting on us for uplift and support.

- **Expand your reach.** Take a moment and think about who is in your inner circle. What value do you add to their lives? Being connected is a mutual benefit and should add value in both directions, but you need to be intentional about seeking out that value. Think about engagement as if it's a romantic relationship. Both parties should be committed to seeing the other grow and move toward excellence. They both should be willing to do what is necessary to make the relationship work. When we get serious about who we are engaging with personally and professionally, we are not only committing to being excellent for ourselves, but we are committing to being excellent for those who are counting on us for uplift and support.

    Being excellent on purpose as an individual will only take you so far. You don't have all the answers and ideas to uncover excellence. Through connecting and sharing your excellence with others—while learning from your partners—you are able to open up new doors. Those doors will give you access to ideas and resources you may not have been exposed to on your own. Cultivating authentic, purposeful relationships is the gateway to excellence. Examine each of your social media relationships and determine what the other person brings to the table—and what you're offering in return. Can you learn more from each person? Are you fully engaging in what they can teach you? Are you offering the full extent of your own excellence to them?

Hardwired Relationships

We literally have the world at our fingertips. There are so many ways to connect with others; however, if your only connections are through social media and you do not take the time to reach out to extend relationships beyond likes, favorites, retweets, hearts, and comments, you are probably missing out on opportunities for purposeful engagement. Most educators who use social media are looking for authentic ways to engage with others, but we need to make sure we're not taking any shortcuts. Be purposeful with how you choose to interact online—which means avoiding the pitfall of just using social media to find an echo chamber or an amen corner. Growth happens when you surround yourself with people who will push your thinking. As you expand your network, add people who don't always agree with your ideas. When you open yourself up to different perspectives or feedback, it gives you the opportunity to make your plan better.

To develop relationships where you feel comfortable with this level of sharing, your connections must also extend beyond the social media platform and become hardwired, or physical. Think of using social media as a catalyst to developing deeper connections with people you may not have had access to otherwise. Think of it too as a way to launch into deeper—and more real-life—connections with those people.

Cal Newport, author of the book *Deep Work*, delivered a TED Talk titled "Why You Should Quit Social Media." The title alone contradicts what I shared in the previous section. While I don't necessarily agree with the major premise of his talk, I was able to relate to some of his key points about building relationships beyond social media. Newport states that "social media is not a fundamental technology." I wholeheartedly agree. It is not the tool that's important here, but what you use the tool to build—the discovery and strengthening of relationships. Once we have made connections and established relationships with others through social media, it is important to enrich and deepen those wireless relationships by making them more accessible and permanent.

This does not mean you should look to connect on a more personal level with everyone you meet on social media. Remember, to *Be Excellent on Purpose* is about finding connections that add value to who you are as a person and a professional. Think of technology as the tool that helps us build wireless relationships that can eventually lead to deeper, purposeful hardwired relationships. For example, if you have found a specific teacher to be someone you follow online for ideas or thoughts on different subjects, reach out to connect in different ways. If the teacher is local, ask about visiting their classroom or meeting up to exchange ideas or share resources.

Hardwired relationships give us the ability to have conversations in real time, unfiltered, and unedited. I have visited many schools, both local and out of my area, as a result of connections via social media. Beyond that, these relationships have helped me solve some of my leadership challenges.

Online and hardwired relationships are both important, and both can serve you well. You can reach out to each other for help and support as needed. You may be able to meet face to face with a few of these connections at conferences, and although social media helps to make these connections, it all starts with a willingness to be vulnerable as we grow our networks of people who make us better. Being connected with educators and people across the world doesn't happen by chance. It happens because we have a need and use the tools available to us to seek others with the same questions, passions, and desires to grow in our craft.

LEADFORWARDSTRATEGY
Deepen Your Connections

- **Engage in face-to-face conversation.** Identify three of your hardwired relationships with people you would call in a crisis. This does not include family. Once you identify these individuals, find the time for a real-time conversation. For example, I meet with a small group of colleagues every month for breakfast. These are personal and professional friends who fill my cup and help me sort through professional challenges. Sometimes we discuss work, but we also discuss our personal lives. The conversation is organic, with no preset agenda. We scheduled the recurring dates and times and put them on our calendars, and agreed with each other that this time is sacred. During these face-to-face conversations, we put technology away so it does not distract us.

  When you engage in face-to-face conversation, I encourage you to choose a time and place where you don't need tech. At the end, reflect on the conversation by asking yourself the following questions:

  - What did we talk about?

  - How was I feeling during the conversation?

- Did the conversation lag?

- Was there an urge to use technology during the conversation to show a visual or make a point?

- Did the conversation add value to my life or help me solve a problem?

This exercise may sound mundane, but what used to be the norm for communication is now becoming a lost art. Carving out time to engage in purposeful conversation with colleagues or close friends helps us build deeper connections with them, which in turn, gives us more opportunities to learn from them.

- **Extend digital relationships into something more permanent.** As I said earlier, it's so valuable to look for opportunities to elevate your digital relationships to in-person connections. Personally, I have digitally connected with educators over ideas and resources on Twitter, Facebook, or Voxer, but when the relationship grew away from social channels and into real life, that's when it truly helped me grow as a person. Expanding those relationships gives us the opportunity to connect with others on a deeper level, and gives us another venue in which to be our authentic selves.

  Are there people among your social media connections whose ideas match closely with yours, or who have experience in completely different realms? How might you physically meet with those people? Conferences are always an option, but if you live close to one another, ask if you can meet for coffee or if you can stop by their classroom or school sometime. Take the first step and move valuable relationships from the wireless realm into the hardwired world.

- **Spend time alone.** We cannot be so focused on connecting with others that we lose the most important connection of all: the connection with ourselves. Occasionally, trade your phone for a pen and a notebook and give yourself the opportunity to reflect. Without checking in with yourself, how will you know what you need? Spending time alone gives you space to explore your innermost thoughts, and gives you the opportunity to focus, rejuvenate, recharge, and recommit to the person you are seeking to be. Staying connected to who you are helps you be available and fully present for others. It gives you the chance to process all of the new things you're learning, and add them to your personal vision of excellence.

  Take the time to just "be" so that you can form your own thoughts and ideas before sharing them. During this time, review your progress on your personal vision and goals. Reflecting on your journey and the wins and pitfalls you have encountered gives you the opportunity to lean into your excellence.

Strengthen the People in Your Network

One morning while taking a spin around my school, I greeted a teacher in the hallway as we passed one another. I noticed that her eyes were watering and her voice was shaky when she said hello. She attempted to move quickly past me and toward the restroom, but I picked up on the cues that something was wrong. Before I was able to mutter the words "Are you okay?" she responded, "I am fine" before bursting into tears. I asked her to meet me in her classroom after she used the restroom.

After the tears stopped flowing, we were able to get to the source of what was upsetting her. Everything that was contributing to her frustration was within her circle of influence, which meant it could be fixed. Just getting her emotions out gave her time to process what she was feeling. By listening to her words and the way she delivered them, I was able to impact her day as we worked together to empower her to solve the problem.

Remember, every encounter you have with someone is a moment of transformation. A common saying among educators is: "People don't care how much you know until they know how much you care." Being able to add value to someone's life means that you have helped them become a better version of themselves, and that increases their ability to impact the lives of others. Take the time to invest in others.

One of the most frequently asked questions is, "How are you?" Most people respond by saying, "I am fine." But how often do those words match a person's body language, facial expression, and intonation? When you ask someone, "How are you?" make sure you really want to know, and that you have the time to listen. To *Be Excellent on Purpose* is not just about growing yourself; it is also about growing others. Building authentic relationships, which means moving beyond surface-level conversations, helps leaders connect with others. Those connections give leaders a chance to lead, motivate, and inspire people toward their own growth—which in turn allows the leaders to grow themselves.

LEAD**FORWARD**STRATEGY
Show You Care

- **Ask probing questions instead of giving definite answers**. When checking in with someone, ask questions that matter. You might have to break through many layers before discovering how someone is really feeling. If you have a relationship and a sense of trust, they will eventually share how they are feeling. Instead of sharing an "If I were you" response, ask questions that will help the person grapple with their feelings. Try using the 5 Whys method (developed by Toyota and now part of the Lean philosophy) in order to get to the core of the emotions. Basically, it means drilling into a problem by asking "Why?" at least five times until the root cause becomes clear.

- **Circle back.** Always check back in with the person. This brings everything full circle for you and for them. It also lets them know that you actually care and have continued to think about them after the initial interaction. Sending a text or email is an easy way to check back in. I also suggest sending a personal note, making a phone call, or setting up a face-to-face visit as more authentic ways of circling back.

MOVING**FORWARD**

When choosing who to engage with, find those who are able to think without limits. We all know the challenges that exist in our profession, but the possibilities to overcome those challenges are limitless if we surround ourselves with the right people. We can't let the system limit our thinking and constrict our connections. If an idea or process is best for kids and doesn't violate the policies and procedures of your current setting, then be open to trying something new. We will never stumble upon those new ideas or plans—or our ultimate excellence—if we don't engage in conversation and connection with people outside our settings.

When we engage with others, we can breathe new life into our ideas, come up with ideas we previously wouldn't have considered, and have our minds blown by the ideas of others. Start small on social media and build your professional network as you become more comfortable. Look for people who think like you, and those who don't yet they have new things to teach you. Look for people who are local to you and those who live on the other side of the world. Think without limits. Engage without fear. Move beyond the conversation. Anchor your engagement on your why and find others who can not only help you grow, but also push and challenge your thinking.

CHAPTER 3
LEAD**FORWARD**JOURNAL

Get connected

Areas where I want to grow:

_____

_____

_____

_____

_____

What social media tools can I use to grow my network?

_____

_____

_____

_____

_____

My closest connected network includes ...

_____

_____

_____

_____

_____

_____

How do these connections add value to my life?

_____

_____

_____

_____

_____

_____

These are ways I invest in my learning and stay connected to self:

_____

_____

_____

_____

_____

_____

What ways can I invest in others?

_____

_____

_____

_____

_____

_____

Share your journal entries and ideas at #LeadForward on Twitter.

Give Focused Feedback

When we give feedback, we notice that the receiver isn't good at receiving it. When we receive feedback, we notice that the giver isn't good at giving it.
— DOUGLAS STONE AND SHEILA HEEN,
AUTHORS AND LEADERSHIP CONSULTANTS

How Can I Help?

NEW AMSTERDAM IS a prime-time show about a doctor who takes over as the medical director of a hospital in crisis. Dr. Max Goodwin comes into a situation with a long list of problems that need to be addressed, ranging from personnel to organizational health to poor leadership. During his first meeting, the body language of a large number of the medical staff is aloof, cold, and uninterested. Their body language demonstrates that they are not committed to making the hospital better for the sake of the patients, which is Dr. Goodwin's number-one priority. It is clear that many of them are not interested in what he has to say, nor do they respect him or his position.

As Dr. Goodwin begins to discuss the state of the hospital and what he will focus on as the new medical director, he calls out the names of departments and individuals that he is terminating because of ineffectiveness or failure to deliver proper care. After these employees are dismissed, the room becomes silent. At this point in the meeting, Dr. Goodwin states his vision for the hospital and asks the remaining staff, "How can I help?" As his staff members begin giving him the feedback he requested, he takes notes. Throughout the series, he takes action on the feedback and makes himself, others, or the organization better.

The primary purpose of giving feedback is to help others grow, and also to help you grow. There is a skill to giving feedback in such a way that others are willing to receive, listen to, and act on it. Think of the saying, "It is not what you say but how you say it that matters." Even when it's tough to give feedback, seeking to be an excellent leader means that you will deliver the feedback in a way that is timely and positive, despite the challenge and discomfort. If you know that the feedback in question will help the organization or individual grow, you must not be afraid to share it. Being committed to helping others become excellent means we step up to the plate and focus our feedback efforts in three areas: validation, refinement, and correction.

Validate. When we think of feedback, we may automatically think about something being wrong. But feedback is extremely powerful when it is used to validate a person, an organization, or an idea. On one occasion, my family and I were all getting new glasses. The associate who assisted us was friendly and patient as she outfitted us in new glasses and processed the paperwork to complete the order. As we came to the end of the lengthy transaction, she asked if we could leave some feedback on Google about our experience. I was more than happy to do it, but if she hadn't asked, I wouldn't have taken the time to do so. I was more than pleased with my experience, which I told her before leaving; however, I had not even thought about giving her written feedback. This experience made me think about the purpose of feedback and the importance of when and how we give it. When we give feedback to validate others, it reinforces what we want to see or experience. How will people know whether their actions have value if they don't receive feedback?

If you are dedicated to being excellent on purpose, there is no way you will be able to ignore inefficient or incorrect behavior. It is preventing you and others from achieving excellence.

Refine. During dismissal one afternoon, I was talking with one of my counselors about an upcoming parent night. She was working on the presentation and mentioned the adjustments she'd made based on notes we had taken the previous year. I only vaguely remembered the notes she was referring to, but clearly remembered the process we went through as a team to gather those notes. After each event, we always focused on what went well and then identified areas where we wanted to adjust for the future. Doing this right after an event or periodically throughout the year gave us the opportunity to make adjustments in the moment, when it was fresh in our minds. Gather feedback to refine your practice and improve yourself and your organization, and give others the same opportunity. This process allows everyone to focus on continuous growth and improvement.

Correct. The most common use of feedback is corrective feedback, which I refer to as checking for accuracy. Corrective feedback should be used when a certain behavior needs to stop and a replacement behavior needs to be implemented.

For example, when a teacher is repeatedly late, the replacement behavior is for them to arrive on time. If a teammate is not pulling her weight on the team and is causing you more work, you need to let her know and assign specific roles. When giving corrective feedback, be sure to state what the person needs to stop doing and what they should start doing. Consider this statement: "Paige, I noticed you have been reporting to work at 8:30 for the past three days. All staff members are expected to be in the building by 8:00 each day." The phrase, "If you see something, say something," is used in reference to safety, but this is true for corrective feedback as well. Address something quickly to keep it from getting any worse.

Giving this type of feedback can be uncomfortable and many people shy away from it and just tolerate the behavior. If you are dedicated to being excellent on purpose, however, there is no way you will be able to ignore inefficient or incorrect behavior. It is preventing you and others from achieving excellence. When you have people committed to being excellent, nothing is more encouraging than working with others who are demonstrating the same behavior. Part of your job as a leader is to make sure you're building an environment where everyone has that same goal in mind, and is building toward it. Remember, excellence and mediocrity cannot coexist. Make excellence the norm.

Reasons to Give Feedback

Validate	Feedback focused on reinforcing what you want to see.
Refine	Feedback focused on making a small, specific change.
Correct	Feedback focused on stopping a behavior or fixing a broken system.

LEAD**FORWARD**STRATEGY
Focus Your Feedback

- **Be intentional about giving feedback**. Look for opportunities to give feedback and make it part of your leadership ritual. For example, each week at the beginning of my leadership team meeting, each participant identifies a staff member they want to recognize. We write a card pointing out something specific we want to appreciate, celebrate, or thank them for doing. This is the first item on the agenda, and we do it right there. After we finish, one of our teammates puts those cards in the boxes. Because of this practice, each of us has become more aware of the importance of validation feedback, and has extended this exercise into our individual practice. This also gives everyone feedback about where they are succeeding and adding value to the organization, which helps them to do more of the same.

    Giving positive feedback is extremely rewarding, and helps our team recognize how the small wins impact the big picture. Where can you give intentional feedback in your own life? Can you incorporate others into this practice? Making it a consistent and organized activity increases the chances of you doing it, and therefore increases the value of the practice.

- **Keep track of your feedback**. Monitor who you give feedback to, and what type of feedback you are giving. If you're only giving feedback in one area, it may mean you are not focusing on the right things. Sometimes we are blinded by what we want to see, and fail to see other things that are in plain view. For example, when a teacher is constantly correcting one student, they may not notice the one time the student actually does the right thing. It is easy to be blinded by the negative behavior we are accustomed to seeing. When that happens, we miss opportunities to promote positivity through validation feedback.

Look for staff members who may be hiding in the shadows. It can be easy to focus feedback on those who are the most outgoing, but as a leader, you must be intentional and equitable when giving feedback to others. Use a spreadsheet to keep track of everyone you have given feedback to, along with the kind of feedback you have given. This will help you see who you may be missing. Also, consider a focus area you want to target and look for ways to give feedback in that area. This helps with supporting progress toward the goals and initiatives of the organization. For example, if your team is focusing on implementing an idea, such as increasing the number of positive referrals given or implementing a new learning strategy, recognize those who are implementing the idea with fidelity. Celebrate their wins and what is working as a result of the implementation. This will support their continued efforts and help others get on board as well. This is also a great way to monitor progress toward the goal.

- **Give feedback a purpose.** Before giving feedback to others, know your purpose. Identify if you are giving feedback to validate, refine, or correct. This will help you frame your words so you can achieve your intended outcome. If you are trying to correct, you need to be specific. If you beat around the bush by starting with something positive, stating what needs to be corrected, and then ending with something positive, it is highly likely that the recipient will focus on the positive parts. The middle of the message sandwich will probably be lost. State the behavior that needs to stop and be clear about the replacement behavior you want to see. Have you ever ended a conversation with someone and walked away not knowing whether they gave you a compliment or criticism? When this happens, the receiver interprets the message in a way that makes sense to them. If you want the feedback to be received the way you intend it, be clear and unambiguous.

It's Not What You Say; It's How You Say It

I am at the stage in my life where I work with teenagers all day, and then I come home to a pre-teen and a full-blown teenager in the evening. They both are wonderful children who provide many blessings to my husband and me, but when they morph into all the weirdness that comes with adolescence, we are unsure who has invaded their bodies and taken command. Teenagers have a way of saying things that provoke great emotion in adults. And if we are honest, it isn't what they say that gets us so worked up; it is the tone and the body language they use when they deliver the message. This is also true of the way we give feedback to others. The way we handle the situation plays a critical role in how they receive it.

If we want to give feedback that produces results, we must practice our skills. Every individual is unique, so every feedback situation will be different. The good news is that the challenges we face as leaders help us develop the right skill set. I am never excited about engaging in a critical conversation; however, I go into each conversation recognizing it as an opportunity to learn. I ask myself, "Why was I put in a position to address this issue?" "What skill set am I sharpening?" "What questions will I use to help reframe this situation?" Then I develop a "pre-game" plan before giving the feedback, so that I'm not only giving the receiver the most effective feedback, but also growing toward excellence.

Feedback Conversation Framework

》》 Identify the area of focus for the conversation.

》》 State the feedback.

> 〉 Use language like "I feel," "I observed," or "Help me understand ..."

》》 Give the receiver time to respond to what they heard you say.

》》 Ask for clarification, if needed.

》》 Reframe or paraphrase what you heard them say.

》》 Close with the following questions:

> 〉 How can I help?

> 〉 What can we commit to?

LEADFORWARDSTRATEGY
Give Valuable Feedback

- **Plan for a feedback session**. Before engaging in a feedback session, be sure to organize your thoughts. Anticipate what the other person might say and have a general idea of how you will respond. I am not suggesting you script your conversation, because that would make it inauthentic. However, it is important for you to be prepared for the many directions in which the conversation could go. That preparation will help you guide the conversation to your desired outcome, no matter the path. For example, when preparing for a feedback session, outline the outcomes of the conversation. Share those desired outcomes with the person receiving the feedback. Use more questions than statements to guide the conversation. Unless the feedback is corrective, use dialogue to engage the recipient of the feedback.

After you have addressed each outcome, summarize the conversation and close with any action items. The person should leave the conversation with a clear path for their next steps. I suggest taking notes on paper rather than on technology, with the permission of the receiver. Both parties should record their thoughts, especially as the other person is speaking, so they can write down anything that comes to mind that they want to share when it is their turn to speak. This will not only help you cover everything, but will also provide a written record to look back on later.

- **Use honest words and be kind.** Assume that people are coming from an honest place—until and unless their actions prove otherwise. Many times, when I have had to give corrective feedback, I've made up a story in my head for why the other person is behaving a certain way. That story is almost always incorrect. Give people the opportunity to become self-aware. More often than not, they will be receptive to what you have to say. They will be even more receptive if you show them that you're seeking to help and not harm. (There are, of course, some exceptions to this rule.) Consider the following phrases to help you emphasize your point:

- Philosophically, we are not in the same place.

- I need to be candid with you.

- This is what I need from you.

- These are my core values and goals for the organization. If you can't give this to me, I am not going to be upset, but we need to explore other options.

- Can you align with me? If you can't, you won't hurt my feelings. We just need to make some decisions.

- As long as you are moving forward and showing growth, I will be patient with you.

- I am sorry this has not been brought to your attention before. Now that you are aware, let's use this as an opportunity to grow.

Using these types of phrases turns the feedback session into a coaching conversation, and as leaders, we are responsible for growing and developing our people. Leave people with their dignity and help them to feel supported.

- **Give tips**. When giving informal feedback, I give it as a tip. I may say, "I like how you wrapped up your lesson. Have you considered giving students time to write their responses before sharing verbally?" or "That was a great strategy you used to teach students how to justify their answers. Here is a tip to consider." Tips are like miniature candy bars. They are just what you need at the moment—not too much and not too little—and they are so good that you can't wait to get another bite. Tips help people improve in the moment because they can be implemented easily and quickly. Best of all, it gives you a chance to offer validation and advice at the same time, in one quick piece of feedback.

Be Careful What You Ask For

Leaders receive feedback from multiple sources. Most of the time, the feedback is unsolicited and can be emotionally charged, especially if it comes from an upset parent or disgruntled staff member. We all have a natural instinct to defend ourselves or those close to us from being attacked, which could prevent us from listening to the feedback that others are giving. It's easy to consider the person giving the feedback as unstable, unhappy, or a troublemaker.

While all of those descriptions may be true, ignoring feedback could mean we're actually missing an opportunity to grow. In the TED Talk "How to Use Others' Feedback to Learn and Grow," Harvard lecturer and author Sheila Heen shared that even though 90 percent of the feedback may be wrong, the 10 percent that's left may be just what we need to focus on in order to grow. We are not obligated to take other people's feedback, but it is important to our growth that we learn how to receive and filter the feedback others give.

Each school year, my staff has the opportunity to give me feedback on what is working and where we can improve, and then ask questions and voice concerns. This is helpful to me and my administrative team because it lets us see what is working for our staff. We also get to address areas that need to be adjusted. The open-ended responses people leave are extremely helpful because they give us specific information. There have been occasions where some of the feedback was hard to accept because it did not seem to be solution-oriented. However, it is important to see past the words and find meaning in some way.

In addition to this feedback, my district uses a culture survey to measure the overall culture and climate of each school. Principals receive a report with charts, graphs, and open-ended comments.

The first year the district offered this survey was my first year at my campus, so I was prepared for the outcome because of the change in leadership. Any time there is a leadership change, there will be mixed feelings about the new leadership. I knew the ratings and comments were more about what was lost than what was new. I viewed each comment and told myself that the overall score would be a baseline, and the lowest it would ever be as long as I was leading the way.

The next year, I was eager to see the results of the report. I felt confident that the scores would be higher, which they were, and that the comments would be favorable—and most were. However, there were some scathing comments that took me by surprise. They were not intended to help our organization get better at all. In fact, they were harsh attacks on me as a person. I was shocked and hurt, and then I became upset. I read them over and over, trying to decipher who would have left such critical feedback. It consumed me for about a week.

After rereading the comments, I began to process the words and filter any meaning out of them that I could. At some point during the school year, had I unintentionally presented myself in a way that would cause someone to view me and my leadership in this light? It did not matter if it was my intent; according to the survey, a few people had received it that way. I tried to replay the school year in my mind to identify that moment in time, but it was impossible. To give myself closure, I pulled out what I could and committed to being mindful of my actions and words to ensure that they did not reflect what the feedback said they did. There was nothing I could do to fix the past, but I had total control over the future. I didn't know what I could do about the specific feedback, but I seized the opportunity to grow and become better.

At the end of the day, each adult in the building owns their morale, but it is my responsibility to create the conditions for a healthy school culture and a climate to thrive. As hard as it was to swallow, I accepted the feedback as someone's reality, whether I agreed or not, and reflected on my practice as a leader. Feedback goes both ways. We must be skilled in giving it and receiving it if we are going to get better. Being able to listen to feedback and grow from it separates those who are satisfied with being good enough from those who are committed to being excellent.

LEADFORWARDSTRATEGY
Look for the Feedback Nuggets

- **Read, breathe, process, and move on**. When you receive feedback, before justifying your reaction, take a moment to pause. We are so quick to respond that we may be missing the tiny nugget of truth, or perceived truth. If you are reading the feedback, jot down questions that you may have about what you are reading. Check your emotions. It is natural to want to bark back if the feedback is negative. Recognize and identify how you are feeling. Process the words and reflect on what someone said. Reflection does not mean acceptance. It means acknowledgment. After processing, if there is something you can take from the feedback, take it and move on. If not, move on anyway. Ultimately, you have to decide to keep it, ditch it, forget about it, or grow from it. As the receiver, you decide, but be sure to choose wisely.

- **Gather feedback in a variety of ways.** To ensure that you have a broad picture from multiple perspectives, provide multiple opportunities throughout the year for people to give you feedback. Informal surveys, focus groups, and casual conversations are great ways to maintain a feel for what is happening in the school.

This also gives you the opportunity to address any concerns or issues that may bubble up.

- **Use protocols to structure conversation.** If you are having a large group feedback session, it is best to use a structured protocol. This gives you the opportunity to organize the conversation so that the feedback is not full of grumblings and complaints that live outside of your circle of influence. This also helps to make the conversation productive and less like a teachers' lounge or parking lot conversation, which usually do not lead to solutions.

MOVING**FORWARD**

The art of giving feedback takes practice and intentionality. As excellent leaders, we need to give feedback and receive it. It is our job to correct and refine, but we also need to remember to praise and reinforce the behaviors we want to see. Feedback is about helping others grow. Both the giver and receiver should be growing as a result of the feedback process. If they're not, one or both parties are doing something wrong. Right around the time I was writing this chapter, I received an email from a teacher I previously worked with at a different school. She was asking me a question about moving into administration and closed her email by saying:

I want you to know that you are the most inspirational leader I have ever had, and I don't know if I have ever told you that. You made me want to grow and be better without making me feel like I was a terrible teacher when addressing the areas I needed to work on. So ... thank you!

I haven't seen this teacher in several years, so to receive this email at the moment I was writing about feedback served to validate the methods I have developed for giving feedback. Even if the strategies I've shared don't work for your leadership style, find a method that *does*. Do whatever you must so that the people you are leading feel like this teacher who emailed me. Remember, feedback is a two-way street. Take turns driving and riding. Both seats are valuable and help you learn and grow.

CHAPTER 4
LEAD**FORWARD**JOURNAL

Give focused feedback

In my weekly practice, opportunities where I can practice giving feedback include ...

_____

_____

_____

_____

My plan for monitoring the type of feedback (validate, refine, correct) I give and how often I give it is ...

_____

_____

_____

_____

Think of a one-on-one feedback session that I need to facilitate. Use the following outline to plan my session:

- The outcome of the meeting is ...

- Based on past experiences with this individual, anticipate possible responses I may hear. Write them down and think about what I would say to each response.

- Write down questions I may want to ask during the session.

- What are potential summary statements I want to say to wrap up the conversation?

- What action items am I expecting to happen as a result of the conversation?

Receive feedback

What are some ways I can gather feedback from others to improve myself and the organization?

_____

_____

_____

_____

_____

_____

_____

_____

_____

How will I process the feedback so that I allow myself to grow?

_____

_____

_____

_____

_____

_____

_____

_____

Share your journal entries and ideas at #LeadForward on Twitter.

Overcome Barriers to Teamwork

It's not about any one person. You've got to get over your-self and realize that it takes a group to get this thing done.
— GREGG POPOVICH, SAN ANTONIO SPURS
HEAD COACH AND PRESIDENT

Engaging in Conflict

"*I* DON'T LIKE CONFRONTATION" is a phrase I often hear when talking with staff members, students, and parents. I don't know many people who enjoy conflict, but I know some who like the drama associated with it. While some individuals love to engage in the action that transpires from conflict, just hearing the word "conflict" makes others uncomfortable. Because of this, people tend to remain silent or shy away from engaging in tough conversations about things that really matter. Past experiences with conflict may have been so bad that people would rather suffer in silence.

Unlike most industries, everything in a school environment is personal, which makes it hard to engage in conflict in an objective way. We spend so much time talking about the importance of building relationships with each other and with the children we serve, how to be nice and kind, and how to work together to support our teammates, while we spend virtually no time discussing how to disagree productively. When the disagreement comes, and it will, we are not ready to engage in productive conflict, which is a conflict that allows all voices and ideas to be heard so the group can develop the best solution.

Getting to this point when working with a team takes vulnerability, intentional effort, time, and reflection. When you prepare for the possibility of conflict, you produce an environment with a free exchange of ideas that includes all voices. And that sort of environment promotes and encourages creative thinking. In this way, productive conflict can actually be a catalyst for innovation.

But you must start by becoming comfortable with some conflict. When you allow others to critique your ideas so you can make the organization even better, it opens you up for learning and new directions, and that leads you into growth and excellence. Avoiding this type of discourse limits your potential to think beyond yourself.

As adults, we tend to focus on completing tasks and projects, and we forget the fundamental principles that we learned in kindergarten: how to play nice in the sandbox with others.

People in schools are excellent at avoiding conflict with others. After team meetings where the group made decisions, teachers usually go back to their classrooms, shut their doors, and do what they feel is best for their students, despite what the team agreed upon. Ideas are often perceived to be owned by the person who suggested them, so an idea may not be considered if it is presented by a teammate who is not as well-liked. This makes the idea playing field uneven, and that does not create an environment where it is safe to share ideas, nor does it ensure that the best ideas are presented.

In fact, it is detrimental to the team because people will realize that the idea is not what is being challenged or criticized, but rather the person sharing the idea. Creating an environment where people matter and feel safe to share ideas is a critical component of engaging in productive conflict. Being able to share ideas and divergent opinions, and discuss them, gives your team the chance to think together and work as a group to solve problems, rather than trying to work individually. Treat conflict correctly, and you give your organization a path toward growth.

Being able to engage in this type of work requires skills that likely we all have learned at some point in our lives. As adults, we tend to focus on completing tasks and projects, and we forget the fundamental principles that we learned in kindergarten: how to play nice in the sandbox with others. Kindergarten teachers teach every social and emotional skill that a child will need to use for the rest of their lives.

- Working with others.
- Apologizing and owning mistakes.
- Showing compassion to others.
- Telling the truth and being honest about feelings.
- Asking for help and helping others.
- Living in peace and harmony.

If you have ever stepped foot into a kindergarten classroom, you know exactly what I am talking about. It is the happiest place in an elementary school. How did we, as adults, forget all of those fundamental skills which are so critical to working in high-performing teams? We can address most of the problems we encounter as teams if we go back to those principles we learned in kindergarten.

In order to practice these principles effectively, we must be good listeners. We have one mouth and two ears. This should mean that listening is important—maybe even more important than speaking. In Stephen Covey's book *The 7 Habits of Highly Effective People*, he speaks about the power of listening. He says, "Most people do not listen with the intent to understand; they listen with the intent to reply." As an individual, if you are only taking in information to respond, you are merely a hearer and transmitter of information. You are not taking the feedback in, and you're certainly not using the point of conflict to brainstorm new ideas. You are hearing to act and not to learn. Being a listener means listening to learn. The Dalai Lama says it best: "When you talk you are only repeating what you already know; but when you listen, you may learn something new."

LEAD**FORWARD**STRATEGY
Listen to Learn

- **Practice active listening.** Listening means taking in information and processing it through several perspectives, lenses, and filters before sharing a response. As educators, listening to learn looks like this:

  - Asking students to give you feedback on your teaching techniques.

  - Recognizing that you have not connected with a student and seeking to understand why.

  - Allowing teachers and other stakeholders to critique your leadership.

  - Owning your mistakes when a team member gives you feedback.

  - Participating in difficult conversations without taking the words personally.

Being able to listen for the purpose of learning, and not for the sake of responding, takes practice. When I am engaging in conversation, I take notes on what I hear. I then repeat those notes back to the speaker and ask them what they would like me to do with the information. If it is about me personally, I ask them what I can do to help them engage in their best work. It is not easy, but I try to separate the message from the messenger. I assume the best intentions from all, and listen through the lens of figuring out what I can do to make the situation better for this person. Sometimes listening without responding is all that is needed. Instead of listening to act in a way that you feel is appropriate, take the time to ask others what they need from you.

- **Share ideas in a structured way.** People who are not interested in pursuing excellence are focused only on their thoughts and ideas, and are unable to hear what others are sharing. To engage in a productive share session, consider the following tips:

  - Agree on what the group is trying to solve and the outcome the group needs to achieve.

  - Give everyone multiple sticky notes so they can write down their ideas. Do this silently so that group think does not derail the group. Silent think time also guarantees that everyone shares their thoughts, rather than just those who speak the loudest.

  - Put the sticky notes in the center of the table and select a person to read the thoughts. It is fine if people remain anonymous during the read-aloud session. This is preferred, so the ideas can be critiqued rather than the people who shared them.

Be Excellent on Purpose

- Discuss the merit of each idea and how it will help the team achieve the outcome you've agreed on. Identify which elements of the ideas you want to discuss further.

Being an active listener and engaging in structured discourse are critical skills for leaders who are committed to excellence. These skills help you lead with excellence, but they also help you grow individually. Listening to learn from others is another way to practice being vulnerable, which opens you up for growth through reflection and refinement.

Learning About Others

Another barrier to teamwork is the idea that we are all individuals and don't need to know much about one another. Unless you are self-employed with a team of one, the majority of your day is spent in a working environment with other people. If you had to stop and jot right now, how much could you write about the lives of each person you work with? I am not talking about deep, dark, personal details, but the names of their spouses or significant others, children and pets, where they are from or live, a small nugget about what they like to do outside of work, an interesting fact, their passions, quirks or fears ... basically, what makes them who they are?

Most people know surface-level information about their co-workers—just enough to have a quick, impersonal conversation. I am certainly not advocating that we reveal our deep, personal secrets and struggles with the people we work with, but I am suggesting that team members take the time to get to know each other on a personal level.

We do not have the luxury of checking our personal baggage at the door when we come to work. No matter how hard people try, we don't have a work self and a personal self. Further, if we don't open ourselves up to sharing part of our personal selves with our co-workers, we will never reach excellence as a team. It is hard to interact with someone you don't connect with on a personal level.

So what exactly do I mean by that? Connecting on a personal level means knowing something about your teammates outside of their work roles. Do they have four young children? Do they sing for weekend weddings? Are they marathon runners or quilters? Do they take care of aging parents? Are they writing a novel? Taking the time to learn the values and styles of the other members of your team creates opportunities to build relationships and fully utilize your team members. It helps everyone, collectively and individually, achieve the excellence we're all aiming for.

Think about your teammates. Can you answer these questions about each individual member of your team?

- Do you know their passion and motivation for the work you're doing as a team?

- Do you know their work personality, and the environment in which they thrive and do their best work?

- Do you know how they like to be approached when you need to address a problem or concern about their performance?

- Do you know how they like to be recognized for their work performance and contributions to the team?

- Do you know their strengths, and areas where they need support?

- Do you know whether or not you do anything that they see as frustrating? Do you know what it is?

Once, one of my colleagues told me that he was having trouble connecting with a specific co-worker. I recommended that he reflect on the D.I.S.C. assessment we all did at the start of the year to see whether it would give him any insight. Once he did, he realized that some of the struggles he was having with this co-worker were actually highlighted on that assessment as personality traits. His co-worker wasn't being difficult on purpose; those were personality traits that were causing a rift between them. Knowing this helped my colleague reframe the thoughts he was beginning to form about his teammate. Understanding more of how his co-worker functioned changed how he reacted, and without that deeper understanding, he would not have been able to strengthen or even work with that relationship. This is the first step toward being a high-performing team. To *Be Excellent on Purpose* as a team starts with each person aspiring to understand their teammates so everyone can work together toward excellence.

LEAD**FORWARD**STRATEGY
Strengthen Yourself and Your Team

- **Identify personality types.** As a leader who is committed to being excellent on purpose, you'll want to understand how your team members think, what motivates them, and what supports or hinders them in doing their best work. Learn about their individual strengths and weaknesses, and reflect on your own as well. No one is perfect. To *Be Excellent on Purpose* means learning how to engage with others in a productive way, and that begins with learning about your teammates. One easy way to do this is with personality assessments, which give you a good baseline understanding of what your teammates are like and how they operate. See the chart for three tools for identifying personality types.

Work Style Personality Assessments

Compass Points	This activity identifies group behaviors we should be mindful of when working together.
D.I.S.C. Assessment	This assessment will help you understand your personality type and work style. This is a great tool for individual growth and a tool to strengthen team performance.
Strengthsfinder Assessment	This assessment helps individuals discover their strengths and talents so they are able to use them to increase self-awareness and improve performance.

After your group has completed the assessments, spend time reflecting on what they mean and what each team member has learned about themselves and others.

- **Identify your balcony and basement moments.** Your best traits are your balcony moments, which occur when you are adding value to the team and others. Think of these as peak performance moments when you make yourself an invaluable teammate. Your basement moments are those less-desirable times when you're not bringing as much value to the team or your teammates. In order to identify your balcony and basement traits, divide a piece of paper into two columns. On the left side, write down the character traits you demonstrate when you are in an environment that is thriving. On the right side, write down the traits you demonstrate when you are in an environment that feels unsafe or unsupportive. Now that you have those traits in mind, draw up a plan for using the balcony traits more often and avoiding the basement traits. The more balcony traits you incorporate in your day, the more valuable you are as a teammate, and the more excellent your team becomes.

The Elephant in the Room

Since we're talking about conflict, let's talk about the conversation in which conflict often happens—and how it can affect the team. I typically have a high threshold for dealing with issues. After processing my feelings and venting my emotions, I am usually able to move forward. However, there was a time in my career when I was not allowing myself to process my feelings and vent my emotions in a positive way. Because I had not dealt with these emotions, I tended to blow up on my team. It didn't take me long to realize that I had to change that if I wanted to be an excellent leader or achieve my vision for myself. I turned to my team and laid out how I was feeling and why, and asked them to do the same.

Although I knew that hearing the feedback was going to be uncomfortable, I also knew it was necessary. I had to invite a discussion if we were going to clear the air and move forward. Talk about a vulnerable moment!

The team was surprised to see my willingness to own my part in our state of dysfunction. As the leader, though, I had to take responsibility for my own actions and figure out how to fix them. Team members who aren't willing to examine their own roles in creating the dysfunction, are part of the dysfunction. We all have to be willing to take responsibility and allow others to give us feedback—even if that means inviting some conflict.

Conflict can be productive when it leads to a positive outcome. People think that avoiding conflict and negative feedback will keep the team comfortable and the environment tolerable. But ignoring conflict leaves it unresolved and means you're not taking advantage of a source of potential growth. Have you ever been on a team where everyone is uncomfortable about something? It's like a giant elephant in the corner of the room that no one wants to mention, much less make eye contact with. If one brave person would just speak on the issue, they would make the first move to banish the elephant. If more individuals spoke, more people would be working as a team to get the elephant out of the room. On top of that, whatever invited the elephant in the room in the first place would begin to be resolved.

Speaking gives the team the strength they need to address and solve the issues that affect them. One person can't remove the elephant, but the strength of the team can. The courageous, productive approach is to launch the uncomfortable conversation and deal with it. You will be a more excellent team as a result.

Since everything is personal in a school environment, we must create a place where it is safe to disagree. Just because we disagree about the work, doesn't mean we have to be in disagreement with the people.

LEAD**FORWARD**STRATEGY
Communicate with Your Team

- **Conduct team assessments.** Team assessments help you to keep a pulse on the status of your team. These assessments give each member a voice and identify areas of strength or concern in a non-threatening way. Even better, they give you a way to have the uncomfortable conversation in a neutral way, rather than in a free-form dialogue that can be misinterpreted. Look at psychologist Bruce Tuckman's work around the four stages of team development to give yourself a framework for these assessments. Focus on giving each team member a voice. Healthy, committed team members who have equal voices build a healthy team, and having multiple people pushing for greatness will keep each teammate growing toward their own excellence.

- **Prepare for the conversation.** Before engaging in a challenging conversation as a team, plan for the following approach:

  - Determine whether the topic of discussion is a problem or a dilemma. A problem has a solution, while a dilemma might not. Categorizing the issue in this way will help the team frame potential outcomes.

  - Set an objective for the conversation. Know the focus and the intended outcome.

  - Check your emotions at the door. Remember that productive conflict is not about you personally. It is about the team and getting the best ideas out on the table.

  - Share your feelings. As a member of the group, you have the right to share your feelings, even if they are different from those of others. As a teammate, you are obligated to speak truthfully. This may be uncomfortable, but remember that silence is a great strategy in these situations. Take a moment before you start speaking to gather your thoughts and figure out exactly what you want to say, to make sure you don't misspeak or leave anything out.

  - Listen without responding. When we listen to respond, we are not focused on receiving the words that are being spoken. Instead, put 100 percent of your focus into listening.

- Work toward an outcome. Aim for closure before everyone leaves the room. Knowing where the team landed on an issue and the next steps they need to take will provide clarity to the group and close the meeting in a way that feels satisfying and productive.

MOVING**FORWARD**

The keys to overcoming barriers to teamwork are getting to know your teammates more deeply, giving everyone an equal voice, and making yourself vulnerable and accepting feedback, even when that feedback is unpleasant. When we focus on the collective instead of the individual, we find ways to use everyone's individual strengths as we seek excellence. At times, this means having uncomfortable conversations and inviting productive disagreement. Allow discomfort in the content of what is said, not in the way that it is said or in a way that fuels discord among individuals.

Leaders must create an environment where it is safe to disagree when talking about the work. Taking time to understand how we work best as individuals and then creating a structure that supports productive conflict and brainstorming within our teams will help us move forward as a group. Instead of maintaining our personal space as individuals, we will be more focused on producing excellent work as a team.

CHAPTER 5
LEAD**FORWARD**JOURNAL

Learning about self

Using the results of one of the recommended personality assessments, consider the following ...

- New learning I discovered about myself from the assessment ...

  _____

  _____

  _____

  _____

- Validation I received from this assessment includes ...

  _____

  _____

  _____

  _____

- One thing I don't agree with is ...

  _____

  _____

  _____

  _____

Learning about others

One way that I plan to learn about the strengths of my teammates is …

_____

_____

_____

_____

_____

_____

_____

_____

_____

When I become frustrated by a teammate, my approach to resolving the conflict will be …

_____

_____

_____

_____

_____

_____

_____

_____

_____

_____

Share your journal entries and ideas at #LeadForward on Twitter.

Be a Champion for Equity

*For most kids in this country, public education isn't their
best shot. It is their only shot. We must get it right.*
— Sir Ken Robinson, International
Advisor on Education

Don't Bless Their Hearts

IN 2016, AT the Texas Association of School Administrators
annual conference, futurist Sir Ken Robinson shared in his keynote address that educators have a duty to address two worlds:
the world of the past and the world of the future that is being created. The students we are charged with educating today will be creating the world of tomorrow.

As this thought settles in, think about the students who come
to school with limited opportunities and experiences. Some of our
children are born into circumstances with limited access to successful examples. Unfortunately, that is an obstacle they must
hurdle before they even step foot into our schools. However, where
a child lives and the circumstances into which they were born
should not determine the type of education they receive. Each day
in schools across our country, many students come to school with

a privilege gap. It is our responsibility to recognize and minimize this gap by creating schools that are focused on ensuring equitable learning environments for all students.

Students should have rich, relevant, and authentic experiences at school, across the board. If every educator in every school pursued excellence instead of allowing excuses about what students can and cannot do, we would meet the needs of all students. Our goal has to be to create schools where excellence is the standard.

For that to happen, however, we have to get away from the "bless their hearts" attitude. "Bless your heart" is a saying in the South that is typically meant to show genuine concern for someone else's well-being ... but also is used to soften the blow of an insulting comment. Too often, it is used in schools to describe a student who is not performing to the standard. You know the type of student I'm talking about: the one also described as underperforming, at-risk, a low achiever, or just plain low. Think about that for a moment.

When an educator is struggling in their craft, seldom do we hear the word "low" used to describe them. We often say they need to be coached up and given additional support and training. We focus our resources, both fiscal and human, on identifying where they need support, and we provide it with fidelity. We monitor and give feedback, and we make adjustments as needed. They are expected to become better educators as a result of this focused, intentional support and training.

But once a student has been perceived to be "low," it becomes a point of no return. Too often, that label becomes the ceiling for that child. Some believe that you shouldn't challenge them by teaching above their heads. Educators begin to talk more loudly and slowly, as if that will make a difference.

We talk about how difficult they are and then bless their hearts, as if that will solve the problem.

So where is the disconnect? We are compelled, almost forced, to provide equitable opportunities for professionals, so why is our profession still struggling to discuss, define, and provide equitable opportunities for our children?

At the 2018 ASCD conference on equity, Baruti Kafele, principal and educational author and speaker, said that when we see what we do as just a job, we believe we cannot save them all. However, when we consider our work as a mission, we become determined to do whatever it takes to create successful students. Their success is our success, and their failure is our responsibility. But we have to believe that about all students, and refuse to leave out those from challenging upbringings. We have to stop blessing their hearts and start having conversations about equity. All children, especially those from marginalized groups, deserve excellent educators in excellent schools. They deserve programs that are designed to help them overcome the challenges and obstacles they face. Education may be their only shot at improving their circumstances.

If inequity exists in your building, be brave enough to call it out for what it is instead of making excuses for it. We need to remove the blinders and stop pretending that inequity doesn't exist in our schools. Equity does not mean everyone gets the same. It means everyone gets what they need. We must shift our thinking away from the current reality of our students and focus on what they will become as a result of our role as educators in their lives.

I wonder what my life would be like now if the people who taught me how to overcome challenges had simply written me off and blessed my heart instead. I was raised in a two-parent home until my parents divorced when I was twelve years old. It was at that time, unbeknownst to me, that I began to experience situational poverty. According to the government, I was living in poverty—and that label went with me into school. At the time, I was searching for the stability, encouragement, direction, and guidance that were missing in my life, and I found them in the teachers and coaches who genuinely cared about *me*, my well-being, and my life beyond school.

Those individuals didn't seek me out because they knew my

situation. No one at school, even my friends, knew my situation. The beauty in the story is that they didn't *need* to know those things to invest in me. What they didn't know was that I needed opportunities and experiences at school more than ever. Those experiences helped me escape from my home life, and I viewed them as a means to a better way of living after I graduated from high school. My education opened doors for me. It allowed me to cross the bridge into another world, which I would not have known if I had not graduated from high school and college. Being a first-generation college graduate helped me to set the stage for my siblings and my future generations.

But it wouldn't have happened if my educators had written me off as a poor kid, given me excuses, and refused to push me into growth. Being in a school that supported me regardless of who I was and where I came from gave me opportunities to grow and reach toward excellence. And every child deserves that same chance. No excuses were made for my circumstances because my teachers knew they were preparing me for life beyond my current situation. Because of the excellent educators in my life, my path was blessed.

LEAD**FORWARD**STRATEGY
Be a Champion for Equity

- **Equalize the playing field.** Look at your school through an equity lens. Conduct an equity walk to examine the following:

  - Are there practices that are exclusionary for some students?

  - Do all students have the same experience at your school?

  - How are students' social and emotional needs being met?

- How do you engage with the families of your students?

First, identify what needs to stop happening, and then you can move forward with equalizing the playing field for all students.

- **Cultivate your impact.** For some children, school and the adults who work in it are the only icons of stability they know. Many of our students have to overcome obstacles and challenges that adults can't even begin to fathom. A person does not have to have the same background or shared experiences to see the sense of urgency in a situation. Our influence is greater than we know, and our impact on the lives of children is substantial—even if we don't share their background. We must get around the labels and use our influence to prepare those children for their future, which is not a world of standardization. We must equip them with tools for contributing to society in their own ways.

  Take advantage of your impact by giving students experiences outside of school so they can begin to see beyond their current situation. Take them on college visits or invite guests from different career fields to come into the school and share the paths they took after school. Learn about your students' cultural backgrounds. Conduct a home visit or tour the neighborhood where your school is located so that you understand the environment in which your students live.

- **Change your practice.** Teach children that their backgrounds won't restrict where they're going. For that to work, you must not only believe it, but also act on it. Take time to reflect on your instructional and disciplinary practices to make sure they are not perpetuating inequity. If what you are doing does not match what you believe, you must stop doing it. Engage in conversations about what you need to change to meet the needs of students, and then create action steps and a timeline to put the plan into action.

When You See Something, Say Something and Do Something

Two words really get under my skin when they are used to describe students and their families: these and those. The words are often used in a way that separates marginalized groups from the expected norms, practices, and beliefs of the majority, as in "those students" don't try very hard, or "these students" bring down our scores. When I became an administrator, I would hear "these" and "those" while reviewing achievement data or working with teachers who were struggling to connect with the families of the children they were serving. When we use those words to generalize students, it removes us from being accountable for the results of our work. We are saying we have no power to influence the situation or the students we are serving. We are saying that we can't change reality for the kids we've classified as "those" or "these," and that we're not willing to make much of an effort.

The words unintentionally push marginalized students to the side, and though they might get something out of the learning, we're not making intentional plans to ensure that they do.

That's not equity. That's not excellent education. And that should violate our most personal and important goal for ourselves: to *Be Excellent on Purpose*.

Instead, use words like "my" and "ours" when discussing your students and families. When you say "our community," "our school," or "our kids," this makes you a part of them. You start to see yourself as being responsible and accountable for their success. Excellent leaders challenge discourse that blames students and their families for their backgrounds. Excellent leaders see it as our moral responsibility to find solutions that meet the needs of *all* students. If the leadership in the school sees inequity and *doesn't* call it out, they're setting a standard—intentionally or not.

It is not easy to call it out, and sometimes it seems that the system is set up for failure, but that does not mean we can give up. We must be committed to challenging any system that sets up barriers for our students. When we change the words, we change our mindsets. And when mindsets change, a change in practice is sure to follow. In their book, *Time for Change*, Authors Anthony Muhammad and Luis Cruz say that "Educators in a healthy school culture believe that all students can excel, and they willingly challenge and change their own practices to meet that end."

If we're truly pushing ourselves toward excellence, we have to take that advice on board and work to make it the truth.

Before we challenge the system as a whole, we must challenge our own beliefs. Our beliefs about the children we serve each day inform our practices. If we have low expectations of our students, we will educate them in a way that produces limited progress and results. This is called deficit thinking, which means allowing student weaknesses to determine our expectations rather than setting our expectations and then using students' strengths to reach them. A child's zip code, race, ethnicity, gender, or intellectual ability should not determine the quality of education they receive. We must start to lift our expectations for all students, and then couple that with support. The bar should be set high, and the only thing that should ever move is the level of support provided for each child.

All students—and I mean *all* students—have strengths and talents. They may not be apparent to them yet, or to you initially, but our job as educators is to help students discover their own talents and strengths and how they can use them to reach their dreams. If they don't have any dreams, help them create dreams. Give them hope, which according to author and speaker Brian Mendler, means "hearing other people's experiences." Try listening to learn and understand before listening to fix and replace.

We must meet students where they are and honor who they are before we can accept the privilege of educating them. Too often, we begin teaching our content to the shells of our students. We are so focused on keeping pace with the scope and sequence and "getting through the curriculum" that we don't even know who is really sitting in our classrooms. In doing so, we're judging them based on the labels that might have come with them, fair or unfair, rather than letting the students tell us who they actually are. We must work to understand that not all students have the same story, even if they belong to the same marginalized group. Remember, equity doesn't mean we have to treat everyone the same way. It means we have to give everyone the biggest opportunity we can, based on who they are and what they can do.

LEAD**FORWARD**STRATEGY
Establish Equity for Each Student

- **Educate the whole child.** The content we teach should be a vehicle to connect with students socially and emotionally. Student achievement is an important aspect of school, but it is not the only education children receive. We need to make our school environments emotionally supportive too, and commit to fostering a culture of efficacy and student agency. When we begin seeing our schools as whole child centers instead of just institutions of learning, we can begin to focus on meeting all the needs of *all* our students. According to the ASCD

Whole Child Approach, a school committed to educating the whole child focuses on the following:

- Ensuring student health and personal wellness.

- Providing a physically and emotionally safe learning environment.

- Engaging students in relevant learning that is connected to the outside world and their community.

- Personalizing learning experiences for students to enhance their self-belief.

- Challenging students academically to prepare them for college, careers, and to be productive global citizens.

Although this is not a tenet identified by ASCD, it is equally important for schools to ensure that the school culture is welcoming to students from diverse backgrounds. Students should see themselves represented in the teaching staff, the resources being used, and the experiences being provided. All students benefit when everyone's culture becomes part of the learning environment. Our society is enriched when we teach from multiple perspectives. Examine your hiring practices to make sure you are seeking diverse candidates to join your staff. Provide equity and bias training for your staff. Create an environment where it is safe to discuss the undiscussable.

- **Take responsibility for student learning.** Some students will learn in spite of us. I call these students "parking lot children," which means they can be dropped off and they will do well regardless of who teaches them. They have a wealth of experiences, privileges, and opportunities, and are well-prepared for learning. However, many students will learn because of what *we* do. Make sure you're building an environment where all students have the same learning opportunities. Some students may be better prepared than others, but it is your responsibility to make sure that they all learn. Get to know your students, figure out what they need, and then spend as much individual time as you can preparing them for that learning.

- **Look at real data all the time.** Achievement data should not be the only data you review. Talk to students about their experiences in school. Ask them if they feel they are treated fairly. Do they have what they need to be successful? Do they feel supported and encouraged to do their best work? Find out what outside influences are impacting their school day. Students are brutally honest and can be one of your biggest areas of insight on whether or not your school is equitable from the student perspective.

Become Conscious of the Unconscious

I was at the 2018 ASCD Educational Leadership Conference on equity when a colleague said to me, "We don't really have an equity issue at my school." I paused before responding, then replied, "Then why are you here?" As we continued our conversation, he shared with me that all the students get along and that all the teachers treat students the same. In making that last statement, my colleague identified his equity issue without even knowing it. When we say we don't have an equity problem, we have just chosen to put on our rose-colored glasses and see everything through the lens of one perspective. As we continued to explore this topic, I encouraged my colleague to ask a wider range of staff and students about the equity in their school, and make a larger study of this area.

He was ignoring the underlying issue—or was, perhaps, completely unaware of it. But that didn't mean it didn't exist.

We all have biases, which means we prefer certain aspects of the world over others. I prefer basketball over football, vanilla ice cream over chocolate, and living in a place that has four definite seasons over a warm climate most of the year. Those are safe bias statements. Our biases become more complicated when we don't recognize that they extend to what we prefer and what we believe about groups of people. In a TEDx talk, "How Do We Overcome Our Biases? Walk Boldly Toward Them," Verna Myers, Netflix vice president of inclusion strategy, says that, "Biases are the stories we make up about people before we know who they actually are."

According to a 2018 report produced by the National Education Association, "Confronting Implicit Bias Through Exemplary Educator Preparation,"[2] implicit bias is made up of the stereotypes and beliefs that we assume are true about different groups of people. It is through this lens that we make decisions about how we will engage with individuals from these groups. According to the report, the beliefs are "unconsciously activated with no provocation by the students." This further illustrates why looking at equity from only one perspective is so dangerous. We only have our own perceptions of others. Handling each person through a single lens is unfair. We have to find a way to see the things we've been unable to see in the past.

In an *Edutopia* blog post,[3] writer Shane Safir shared a story about how she tried to advocate for the students she was working with at a diverse urban school. She was pushing her students to produce work that was preparing them for what they would see at the collegiate level. One of her students asked her why they were not receiving advanced credit for the course when they were working so hard. She agreed and appealed to the administration on their behalf. She was told that the students in her school were not "accelerated enough to handle honors curriculum." Unfortunately, this storyline is repeated in schools across our country every day. In this situation, it didn't matter what the students were demonstrating; the decision had already been made that they were only going to reach a certain level because of their background, and that bias was truth in the minds of the leadership.

Implicit bias is prevalent in our schools and classrooms and is often the invisible glass ceiling that prevents educators from realizing their potential to inspire and impact the lives of the students they serve. It robs students of what they could be because the adults in the school are unable to recognize how their own biases are impacting how they relate to the children. The beliefs and attitudes of educators greatly influence the students they serve, both positively and negatively.

Be careful not to let your implicit bias and perspective about your students push them toward the stereotypical paths that society has perpetuated. More importantly, do not push them away from ideas or issues that are a part of who they are. Students should not have to hide or diminish who they are culturally to fit into the school environment. If you don't understand something about a student culturally, seek to learn. Ask a trusted colleague. Engage in research. The best way to get to know students culturally is to get to know them individually. Know who you are serving.

LEAD**FORWARD**STRATEGY
Get Comfortable Being Uncomfortable

- **Identify your bias.** Be brave and acknowledge that you have a bias. Acknowledgment is the first step in waking the unconscious beliefs that we all hold about others. Take a moment to take the Implicit Association Test, which was developed by professors from the University of Washington, University of Virginia, and Harvard University. The purpose of this assessment is to learn about the bias we hold as it relates to groups of people and ideas. Many times, people are afraid to say what they really believe about others, or they may be completely unaware of what they believe to be true. The work of these professors extends to Project Implicit (implicit.harvard.edu), which is a nonprofit organization dedicated to the study of implicit bias, diversity, and inclusion. This is an excellent resource and a great place to begin your journey in this area. Once you identify your bias, make a commitment to challenge and change your thinking. Explore ways to engage with others from different backgrounds. Read and study the history of different cultures. Be vulnerable and immerse yourself in learning about others.

If it is important to us, we will find a way to ensure that all students have a safe, supportive, equitable environment to thrive academically, socially, and emotionally.

- **Become a student of culture.** It is common in our society for people to immediately think about race and ethnicity when we hear the word "culture." Culture is not race. In fact, there is much more to us than our race and ethnicity. Unfortunately, society has used the social construct of race to sort and divide groups of people, and because of that, we may have limited knowledge and beliefs about people who are different from us. Learn about the values, social norms, beliefs, and practices of others. Broaden your circle. Remember when we learned about expanding your connections in Chapter 3? If everyone around you looks like you and has similar experiences, then extend your reach and find others to include in your circle.

If we don't challenge our beliefs by understanding the culture of others, then it doesn't matter what systems, pedagogy, or curriculum we put into place. There is nothing wrong with the brains of our students, but unless we examine the culture in which the brains are learning, we are setting ourselves and our students up for unnecessary struggle and setbacks. Be genuinely interested in experiences that are not your own. There is more to the world than your perspective, and when we recognize this, we can begin to view the world from a different set of eyes. Understand the community and children you serve and don't make excuses for things you don't know or understand. Be intentional when extending your connections so that they meet the areas of growth you are exploring.

MOVING**FORWARD**

I believe the biggest challenge principals face today is the fight to eradicate inequity. We have been using standardized testing to sort and separate children for two centuries, and we have been "reforming" public education for years by making sure we don't become a nation at risk by leaving children behind, as we race to the top to ensure that every child succeeds. However, through all these things, the issue of equity for all still remains.

The battle for equity fuels my passion as a leader. For many students, their only chance at a better life is through receiving a quality education. External forces such as policy mandates without funding, implicit bias, low expectations, the political climate, and racial and social injustice all manifest themselves in the schoolhouse each day. Through all of those issues, leaders are responsible for ensuring that students are receiving an exceptional education in a supportive environment that promotes equity for all. There is no silver bullet to solving inequity issues. The only way to help leaders with this cause is to be a champion for *all kids*.

In order to change the narrative of this story, each leader must be courageous in the settings in which they are charged with leading. When we see inequity, we must call it out for what it is. We can't remain silent. We must be a voice for the voiceless and an advocate for those who can't or don't know how to advocate for themselves. We must give hope to the hopeless. Inequity is robbing students of the best experiences they could ever have if we are not courageous about addressing it when we see inequity in education. Even if we have students or teachers who don't believe in themselves, we must always believe in the possibility and potential of every teacher and every student. Being courageous and hopeful won't amount to anything if we don't move beyond the conversation. We must put feet to our words by developing plans that intentionally challenge, address, and eradicate inequity. If it is important to us, we will find a way to ensure that all students have a safe, supportive, equitable environment to thrive academically, socially, and emotionally. If not, this conversation will continue.

You decide. The choice is yours.

CHAPTER 6
LEADFORWARDJOURNAL

Identify your bias

Take the implicit bias test at https://implicit.harvard.edu/implicit/takeatest.html. Be open to what the results say, even if you don't agree. After taking the assessment, reflect on the following:

- I was most surprised by ...

  _____

  _____

  _____

- Before the test, I used to think _____

  _____

  _____

- Now I think _____

  _____

- One way that my bias has impacted my ability to connect with students and colleagues is ...

  _____

  _____

  _____

- I plan to challenge my thinking and beliefs about people who experience life from a different perspective than I do by ...

  _____

  _____

  _____

Look at your school through an equity lens

Using different forms of data (achievement, behavior, social, emotional), identify the names and faces of students who:

- are not achieving at the same level academically as their peers (achievement)

- are frequently sent to the office for disciplinary reasons (behavior)

- are underrepresented at your school (social and emotional)

After you have identified the students, respond to the following questions:

- What are we doing that is preventing our students from achieving at the same level as their peers?

　
_____

- Why are certain students sent to the office more frequently than other students?

　
_____

- How are we meeting the needs of our students who are underrepresented on our campus? Identify specifically what is being done to ensure that students are included.

_____

- How do you know that your actions are effective?

_____

Share your journal entries and ideas at #LeadForward on Twitter.

Lead Impactful Change

When you change the way you look at things,
the things you look at change.

— WAYNE DYER, AUTHOR AND SPEAKER

Balcony View

IN RONALD HEIFETZ and Marty Linsky's book *Leadership on the Line*, the authors speak about the importance of viewing your organization from the balcony instead of from the dance floor.

Leading from the balcony means seeing the big picture. When I started my journey at my current campus, I spent a great deal of time on the dance floor. It was hard to see what was going on during the dance since I was on the floor. My view of our organization was solely dependent on the partner I was dancing with at the time. This became frustrating because every dance partner had a different perspective that often collided with the others I had previously heard.

Viewing from the balcony gives the leader perspective about who is on the dance floor and how well they dance and who they choose to engage with during the party. Changing my view from the floor to the balcony gave me the opportunity to identify areas where I needed to focus, as well as key players who would be critical in helping me move my vision forward. From the dance floor, I felt that change would be virtually impossible because there was no clear path through the many people on the floor. When I changed my perspective and was able to see everything, I could see quite clearly what needed to be done. This gave me the insight I needed to lead and implement growth.

The importance of being able to see things from a different perspective became even more evident when I went on a historical tour. After we finished a project in Washington, D.C., my colleagues and I decided to do a quick night tour of some of the monuments. This was my first experience in D.C., so I was excited and overwhelmed by all the history around me. When we got to the Lincoln Memorial, I stood in that space, speechless. The memorial was absolutely phenomenal, and the view from the steps allowed my eyes to see the two-mile stretch to the Capitol. I stood at the same spot where Dr. Martin Luther King Jr. stood when delivering his "I Have a Dream" speech, and got a glimpse of what it may have felt like to look out and see people as far as the eye could see and deliver that powerful message.

Here's the connection: Dr. King managed to see things from both the dance floor and the balcony. Despite what was going on in cities across the country and in other parts of the world, he stayed committed and focused on his vision of equality for *all* mankind. Although he worked in the trenches alongside others during the civil rights movement, he never lost sight of the bigger picture. He led from the balcony, and when necessary, he left the balcony and made his way to the dance floor. He was connected in both areas, which gave him the perspective he needed to impact lasting change.

LEAD**FORWARD**STRATEGY
Plan for Change

- **See the big picture**. Don't let yourself get caught in the weeds. If you do, you won't be able to see the beauty of the whole garden. Be sure to gather information from many sources. Find out what is working well and identify areas that need more attention. You don't have to focus your attention on everything all at once. Seeing the big picture allows you to see which areas cross over and impact others. Work on areas that you can impact in the greatest way. Prioritize your plans and focus on the quality changes that will make a lasting impact rather than quick changes with short-term gains that will not be sustained over time.

- **Ask more questions than you give answers.** We all know that change is hard. Asking a number of questions before making a change can be even harder. In my experience leading change, when I ask questions to gain an understanding of a situation, people often get uncomfortable. Asking questions can come across as questioning someone's practices, beliefs, or motives. The way you frame questions is important if you want to be able to truly understand the journey of an organization. (For an in-depth look at the art of asking questions and how to create a school culture of inquiry, see Connie Hamilton's book *Hacking Questions*, part of the Hack Learning Series.)

Leaders who are excellent on purpose know how to use shared leadership to get everyone on board when it comes to growing and changing.

Ask questions as if you are writing a feature article. This gives people the opportunity to talk freely as they share the highlights of their programs or initiatives. Possible suggestion frames include:

- I know you are proud of the many accomplishments of your school. Tell me about the journey. Where were you and how did you get to where you are now?

- What are the things you are most proud of? Why?

- What challenges do you currently have? Do you have any ideas about how to overcome those challenges?

- What words of advice would you give to someone wanting to implement the same change on their campus?

- What areas would you like to see improved?

These question stems are not threatening, and give those responding the opportunity to reflect. If people are able to identify for themselves the areas where change is needed, it makes it their change, rather than a change you requested of them. According to Dr. Rob Evans, clinical and organizational psychologist, it isn't that people don't like change; they just don't like someone else's change. When possible, help people to believe and understand that they own the change. Leaders who are excellent on purpose know how to use shared leadership to get everyone on board when it comes to growing and changing.

- **Develop a written plan.** Have you ever been part of a change initiative that was poorly planned and executed? I have, and it is extremely frustrating. Before beginning the change process, develop a written plan that you can share with all parties involved. People need to know where they are going and how they will get there. When I moved to my second principalship, I developed an entry plan that looked something like this:

- Commit to researching your school during your first year. Look at multiple measures of data, both quantitative and qualitative.

- Use surveys to get insights from all stakeholder groups.

- Observe the school climate and dig into the school culture.

- Identify groups you plan to meet with as well as the questions you will ask during the interviews.

- Create a timeline that outlines the activities you will engage in during the year.

- Share your findings with the staff and community.

- Use your plan to determine the next steps. This will guide your work and keep you focused on the outcomes you are seeking.

Re-Learning How to Ride a Bike

Unlearning what you have always known is a difficult task. Although we utilize our previous knowledge and skills as anchors when we learn something new, it is hard for some people to link previous learning to new ways of doing things. When I was an elementary principal, our data revealed that we needed to change the way we were teaching math. The teachers had the knowledge about what needed to happen, but they didn't understand the process for implementing the change. In order to move from knowledge to action, we had to practice our learning instead of being terrified by the thought of learning something new.

The best example of this happened a few years ago during a principal's meeting. We watched *The Backwards Brain Bicycle* video on YouTube. In this video, Destin Sandlin explains how he learned to ride a backwards bicycle. Sandlin is an engineer and he worked with welders who liked to play jokes on the engineers. One of the welders switched the handlebars on the bike so that when you turned the handlebars right, the bike went left, and when you turned the handlebars left, the bike went right. Sandlin took the challenge, thinking the backwards bicycle would be easy to control, but quickly learned that it was virtually impossible to ride the bike. His brain had been trained to use one algorithm when riding a bicycle, and it was hard to reverse it. The brain had to completely unlearn what it had learned about riding a bike. After eight months of daily practice, he eventually learned to ride the bicycle.

But what is interesting is that he forgot how to ride a normal bike.

When we are leading change, we are asking people to stop doing something they know and feel comfortable doing so they can learn something new. Sandlin was able to relearn how to ride a regular bike in less time than he had learned how to ride the backwards bike because of his years of previous practice. His brain clicked right back into that algorithm. Reverting back to old habits is easy to do. Think about how easy it is to stop a workout regimen or abandon a diet. Successful change happens when the new behavior becomes the new normal and you can't imagine doing it a different way. The way it used to be served a purpose for a moment in time, but when we learn a new way that is more effective and efficient, it makes sense to begin using the new strategy. Many principals tried to ride the metaphorical backwards bicycle in our meeting that day. All of them were unsuccessful, because learning how to do something new takes time and intentional effort.

Change is a double-edged sword. For some, it is exhilarating and exciting, and for others, it represents loss and grief. As leaders, we cannot lose sight of that when we're talking with others about change. Understanding that what people do is what defines them will help you understand why asking them to change can be hard. Asking people to change can make them feel incompetent, or like they are being disloyal to the person who helped them get to where they are. Challenging ideas can feel like a personal attack.

Yes, change is hard, but it's necessary for growth, for pursuing excellence, and for doing the best you can for your students. It is your job as a leader to make change a clear path for your people, so they know exactly where they are going. It is unfair to expect people to follow you if you have not given them a clear path ahead. Good leaders find out *why* people are scared. Excellent leaders figure out *how* to get around that fear and make it easier for people to move.

LEAD**FORWARD**STRATEGY
Lead Your Team into Change

- **Identify the challenges.** Before initiating change, identify what *kind* of change the organization will be facing. According to Heifetz and Linsky, there are two types of challenges: adaptive and technical. Technical challenges are easier to overcome because they do not involve letting go of something that is deeply rooted in your work or who you are as a person. These challenges have relatively easily implemented solutions. An example of a technical challenge could be changing the dismissal process. Changing this system can be done easily, and few people will have a feeling of loss over it. Adaptive challenges, however, include making fundamental changes to practices, values, and beliefs. There are no easy solutions to this sort of change. As leaders, we need to be transparent when we communicate the types of changes we will be leading. This type of transparency will help everyone to be prepared for the process.

- **Go on a listening tour.** Learn about the past before you begin to shape the future. A listening tour involves one of the most critical skills a leader can possess: the ability to listen to others without passing judgment or offering solutions. By nature, leaders are problem-solvers and fixers. They see things that can be done better, and they want to put a plan in place immediately to improve things. When you walk into a new leadership role, it's so easy to see things that others who have been inside the organization cannot or choose not to see. What may be obvious to someone with fresh eyes or a different perspective may be wallpaper to those who have been on the inside for some time. The wallpaper may not even be pleasant, but since it is familiar, it is safe.

When a new leader begins to question the choice of the wallpaper, such as the color, pattern, or texture, people start to pay attention and notice what they may not have noticed before. This is where listening comes into play. When you're filling a new role, let those you will be leading know that you will be asking questions to understand where the organization has been so that you will know how to plan for where it will go next. Tell them that you're going to ask a lot of questions and that you need their feedback. Once you've gathered their feedback, you'll be able to start planning for the change.

- **Give time and support, and stay the course.** It is vital to give time and support throughout the process. Once you've decided on what you want to change, let everyone know that they've got time to get used to it. Putting pressure on them to change without giving them time or support just sets them up for failure. Realize, too, that you're going to come up against the "invisible we." This includes people who make statements such as "Everyone is struggling with this new change" or "I hear people are not happy with the changes you're making." Instead of taking the words of the "designated spokesperson" for the group, ask them to identify who makes up "everyone" and "the people" they are referencing. If specific people are unhappy, do what you need to do in order to support them. During change, you cannot let vagueness and ambiguity hijack your emotions.

Ownership Versus Buy-in

In his book, *The Principal: Three Keys to Maximizing Impact*, author and educational consultant Michael Fullan discusses the importance of focusing on using the right drivers during the process of change. Leaders must challenge the status quo, and also have a plan for *how* to change the status quo. Work to understand the group dynamics of the people you will be leading through the process. When leading a change, you'll come into contact with three types of people: those who love and are thrilled with the change because they see the need for it, those who are against it because they have to lose something in order for the change to occur, and those who are indifferent and have no opinion about it.

Leaders must be able to clearly articulate why the change is needed, the implementation plan for the change, and the plan for building capacity (the process of developing and strengthening the skills and processes the organization needs) if they want to take these groups into account and move the change forward. Building capacity in others begins with an active relationship. Without any relationship, there is no ownership, and the best you can get is buy-in, which can be temporary and fleeting.

Think of it this way. Let's compare buying a home versus leasing a home. If I choose to lease a home, I only plan to be there temporarily. My monthly payments are paying the mortgage for the homeowner, and there is no return on investment to me as the tenant. If the home needs repairs, the landlord pays for them, and I don't have to pay for any upgrades. The headache is not mine. Actually, it is somewhat freeing to call someone else to deal with the problem. I am hands-off when it comes to fixing issues. At some point, either I or the landlord can terminate the relationship, and I can walk away. Choosing to lease a home means I am willing to try it before I make any decision about living there permanently.

If I choose to purchase a home, on the other hand, it is mine. I am responsible for everything that comes with running a home, which includes repairs, upgrades, and the surprises that owning a home brings. In this case, I'm committed to a very large financial endeavor from the beginning.

Leasing is equivalent to just buying into an idea or initiative, and owning is equivalent to being committed to the idea and initiative from the beginning. When working with others, I want ownership over buy-in. Ownership means that individuals are committed to seeing the idea thrive and will do what they need to do to make it work. They will find solutions to problems and think through potential threats to success. Even after the leader is gone, the idea or initiative will continue to thrive because each member of the group owns the work. Buy-in is a result of position and timing. Usually, when someone says they will buy into the idea, they are convinced but not committed. These individuals will go along with the idea, but as soon as the opportunity presents itself to go in a different direction, they'll abandon the initiative.

Excellent leaders make it their priority to lead lasting change so that the work continues long after the leader has left. The work should be owned by the organization, which only happens when it is cultivated through building capacity in others. One leader, in particular, had a great influence on me professionally because she stood firm in her why and purpose. Many of my colleagues, myself included, still quote her words of wisdom and utilize her vision as a blueprint for our instructional leadership. She built capacity in others so that her work carried through every thread of all that was done in our organization. Even though I have not worked with her in over ten years, I own the work that she led as my own, and it is prevalent in my work as a leader today. She not only built capacity in others, but also took the time to build relationships. She was an excellent leader who helped her entire team grow.

Capacity building means ensuring that teachers, students, and parents are ready to thrive beyond their current setting. Capacity should transfer to different situations. Think beyond the current setting to a place where individuals will use what you taught them in a setting that will benefit them beyond the classroom context.

LEAD**FORWARD**STRATEGY
Jumpstart the Plan for Commitment

- **Challenge the status quo.** If we aren't helping students grow academically, socially, and emotionally, we must stop doing what we are doing, and change things. It is easy to get comfortable with the systems and structures in place at our schools, but if they are only working to meet the needs of most and not all, then they must be redesigned. Doing what has always been done is safe for the adults, but we must challenge the status quo and change to meet the needs of the students if we're going to be excellent educators. We must have a commitment from the members of our team. Together, conduct a S.W.O.T. analysis (Strengths, Weaknesses, Opportunities, and Threats) to determine where to start. Consider the following steps:

  - Identify the strengths of your organization. What is working and why?

  - Examine the weaknesses. Where are you missing the mark? What do you need to stop doing?

- Discuss the opportunities for failure. Remove the blind spots to determine where the organization has the potential to fail.

- Determine the threats to the organization. What obstacles could derail your progress?

Once you find the status quo in your school, develop a plan to move your systems toward excellence. Plan for the pitfalls and pushbacks. Be committed to the process and stay the course.

- **Communicate a sense of urgency but provide support.** We all know the work that we do is vital to student success and well-being. What we do as educators becomes more complex each year. For many children, education is their gateway to a better life, and we must not lose sight of this. As you lead your school, remember to communicate a sense of urgency, and share the why for the change. Also, provide support to create a commitment, to help the staff implement the change, and to give your organization a better shot at success. Anticipate where your staff may struggle and ask them what support they need from you as they go through the change process.

- **Plan for excellence.** Unless you have a plan that includes goals, timelines, and measurements of success, your intentions are just words. As you lead the change, see yourself where you want to be and develop steps and action items to get there. Think about what your organization needs to do to grow beyond the current state and find the resources you need to support the change. Write it down and pass it out. Putting it on paper and sharing it with the team increases ownership and gives them a chance to give you feedback and help brainstorm new ideas. Build incremental checkpoints into the plan to allow you to measure progress and make adjustments along the way.

MOVING**FORWARD**

We respond to change based on what the process means to us personally. According to psychologist Rob Evans, our brains are wired for patterns, and patterns give our lives meaning. Therefore, even if the change makes logical sense, it may be hard, psychologically, for the person who actually has to accomplish it. Most people resist change they did not create, and that is normal and necessary.

Change can represent a loss. For some people, it means throwing out what makes sense to them in order to learn something new and unfamiliar. They may perceive this as a necessity so they can become the person you want them to be. They may internalize this as you saying they are not good enough, which leads to feelings of incompetence. Change doesn't mean that what was done before wasn't good work. It may have been good for the time in which it was created, but for our current reality, it is not working. The organization should have a clear understanding of the why, what, and how of the process of change so they can understand and own the new work they are being asked to do.

As you lead change in your organization, clearly communicate the non-negotiables and apply support and pressure to make the change. The way you initiate and lead the change will determine how successful the process will be for your organization. Lead wisely!

CHAPTER 7
LEADFORWARDJOURNAL

Leading change

Reasons I am proposing this change initiative ...

_____

_____

_____

_____

_____

_____

Three steps that I will take to lead effective change are ...

- _____

- _____

- _____

My plan for communicating the change is ...

_____

_____

_____

_____

_____

_____

_____

_____

_____

_____

In order to measure if the change I am leading is effective, I will ...

_____

_____

_____

_____

_____

_____

_____

_____

Share your journal entries and ideas at #LeadForward on Twitter.

Amplify Student Voice

It is not enough to simply listen to student voice. Educators have an ethical imperative to do something with students, and that is why meaningful student involvement is vital to school improvement.

— ADAM FLETCHER, WRITER AND SPEAKER
FOCUSED ON YOUTH VOICE

Listen to Learn

As EDUCATORS, OUR end users are the children we serve each day. Without them, we wouldn't have jobs. If you really want to know what is going on in your school, talk to your students. They will be candid as they share their experiences, and most of the time, they will offer solutions they think will work. In my school, when there is an area where we need to improve, I've often started with ideas from students. Remember the strategy from Chapter 4 where I shared the importance of gathering feedback in a variety of ways? Nothing is more powerful than allowing your students to be part of this practice.

As you listen to them, remind yourself that you are listening to learn. Don't try to defend what they are critiquing. The point is not whether you agree. The point is to listen to learn, and to improve the school. If your students are sharing the way they see the situation, it gives you a new view—and another way of thinking about a problem. Seeing you asking for feedback and taking action on their ideas also teaches the students how to listen to others. You are showing them what it means to be excellent by constantly seeking to learn and grow.

Excellent leaders know the importance of leaving their balcony view not only to get on the dance floor with the adults, but to engage with students as well. Just recently, while chatting with a group of students, they updated me on issues in the school, where the students were struggling or excelling academically or personally, and on things they wanted to bring to my attention. The conversation was so organic and comfortable that I could have talked with them all day. These are the experiences that should encourage us as educators. Students should feel comfortable talking with us. When our students see us as advocates and mentors for them, we can help them grow and mature.

If we want to be the types of leaders who fill that role, we must be visible and present in the spaces students occupy. We need to be approachable and genuinely interested in who they are and what they are saying to us. We must ask questions that will help us understand their experience and how to make it better. We must be equitable in our questions, and open to their feedback. If you are not getting feedback from your students, you are missing a gold mine of knowledge about the culture and climate of your school.

In addition to the informal conversations, think about how you can involve students in more structured discourse that gives you the feedback you need to ensure that your school is meeting the needs of your students. For example, select students from multiple demographic backgrounds to work with you in an advisory role. This group on my campus serves as my Principal's Roundtable. During all of our meetings, we collaborate and plan ways to make our school better. There is always space on the agenda for us to discuss "issues." During the issues section, I allow students to express the concerns they have with our school. If the issues section is not given ample time, my students let me know that we need to dedicate more time to it in our next meeting.

The students love this part of the meeting because they have the ear of the principal. In their minds, I should be able to fix everything they perceive to be an issue. Most of what they discuss is within the realm of our control as staff members. They also point out inconsistencies in areas and items of concern they observe among the student body. On one occasion, the students shared with me that we had a serious problem with the use of technology. Students were addicted to their phones, and something needed to be done because they were not fully present during learning time. They said that seeing other people on their phones distracted them while they were trying to learn. Yes, this came from the mouths of students!

We need to stop assuming that as adults, we know everything about what our students are thinking and what they need. While our wisdom rules in many areas, we still need to involve our students in the conversation.

I shared this with the staff and we discussed our role in helping students manage their technology and refined our campus process. Students want structure and guidance, and they depend on us to give it to them. We need to stop assuming that as adults, we know everything about what our students are thinking and what they need. While our wisdom rules in many areas, we still need to involve our students in the conversation.

Another way to amplify student voice is to facilitate a student panel. I have done this at both the elementary and the secondary levels. Most recently, I met with a student panel comprised of students who were members of the PTSA. I asked them the following questions:

- What is going well at our school?
- What do they like most about our school?
- What are some areas we can improve in our school?
- What is something that they really want me to know?

Listening to students and taking notes gives you valuable feedback on what is going well and where the school needs to improve. Listening to students is the first step. Take their feedback and do something with it to show them that their voices have the power to make a difference. More importantly, follow up with them when they come and talk to you about their concerns. If you don't know the answer to their question, tell them you will get back to them once you have had the opportunity to gather the information.

Also, have an open-door policy for your students. Give them the opportunity to make appointments to share a proposal or an idea. But do not allow students to leave a problem or idea in your lap if they have the power and influence to address it. Give them the opportunity to implement their idea and help them make it a reality, if possible. Teaching students how to advocate for what they want gives them an important life skill. Be an advocate for students by doing whatever is necessary to make sure they have a great experience at school, and create the conditions where they learn how to advocate for themselves.

LEADFORWARDSTRATEGY
Amplify Student Voice

- **Make yourself available and accessible to students.**
  Try to be around them as much as possible. Engage with them. Think about how a manager at a restaurant

interacts with customers in the dining room. They want to make sure the dining experience is exceptional, and they seek to satisfy any need the customer brings to their attention. The same approach can be used when talking with students. You must be among the students to get the authentic, honest feedback that truly makes a difference. Just as a coach can't coach from the locker room, the principal can't lead from the principal's office.

- **Conduct student panel discussions or focus groups**. To extend the informal conversations to a more structured format, consider using student panels or focus groups to inspire deeper conversations with students. This structure gives you the opportunity to select a broad range of voices to participate. It also helps you to focus the conversation on the type of feedback you want to gather. For example, I asked teachers to identify one student who challenged them the most behaviorally or academically. I was able to have one-on-one conversations with these students about what their school day looked like. I was sure that if the teachers didn't know how to meet the needs of their most challenging students, there had to be frustration on the student end of the relationship. This focused conversation gave me the information I needed to help teachers grow in this area, and allowed me to show the students that I was committed to making the school environment one in which they felt supported.

    If you want a larger focus group to work with, select students who can speak to the subject you are exploring. For example, if you want to learn about how a program is being implemented across the school, pull students from each grade level. Also, be sure that the students you select represent the demographic makeup of the school. Equity is always a critical component when assembling focus groups. You want to make sure that the group represents multiple voices and perspectives. A focus group is a closed-session meeting between you and the students. This creates a safe environment for students to share freely. Even so, select students who do not mind speaking in front of others. Also, be sure that your panel does not have too many student participants (no more than ten) so that airtime is equally shared.

- **Use surveys to gather student perspective.** When you give every student the opportunity to share their voice, you can make adjustments based on a larger set of suggestions. When developing your survey, include open-response questions in addition to multiple-choice. This gives students the opportunity to extend their answers to include more meaningful responses. This also gives you the opportunity to collect data in a variety of ways.

Discover Their Motivations

Encouraging students to share their voice helps them be more committed and connected to the learning environment. Far too often in schools, we make most of the decisions for our students. We tell them what to do and how to do it and ask them if they have questions about our instructions. It is not the norm to put students in charge of their learning. We tell them what they scored on an assessment, point out everything they did not do correctly, and tell them what they need to fix for the next assessment.

I have a news flash, educators: Before your students take the assessment, they already know what they are going to miss. You might explain what they did wrong and what they should have done to get the correct answer, but your words are going in one ear and out the other.

We need to start including students in the educational process. Students need to be active participants in setting and tracking learning goals. Without setting goals for their learning, how will they know when they are learning and improving? Furthermore, if students are involved in setting and tracking their goals, they will take ownership of their learning and be more invested in the process. We certainly cannot rely on grades to be the only measure of growth. Goals should be collaborative decisions made by the teacher and the student, and include various measurements and progress checks along the way.

Through goal-setting, students become owners of their learning. With the guidance of their teachers, they begin to understand what the standards mean for them. If their teacher gives them scaffolding and support, they have a clear path to move toward improvement and excellence. Instead of telling students what to do, give them tools for self-evaluation and reflection, as well as a place to collect evidence that demonstrates their progress toward the learning standards. Give them ownership in the process. (For a quick read about how to create a contemporary curriculum, see *Hacking Instructional Design* by Michael and Elizabeth Fisher.)

Goal-setting also helps students to become more aware of the learning that teachers expect them to experience. They'll use that awareness to become more engaged in the process itself. Without goals, their motivation and engagement decrease, because they don't see where they're supposed to be going, or what their part might be in that journey. Start goal-setting with your students, and include individualized, targeted feedback. As we learned earlier, focused feedback leads to improved practice. Give the students the tools they need to dictate their own goals, and then give them the support they need to reach those goals, and you're helping them move toward excellence.

Refine this process by choosing a limited number of goals so you can focus on the most important needs of your students. Limiting the number of goals will help students focus on the most critical areas of learning. Help each student choose their own goals, and start them at an entry point that is challenging but attainable. When students experience success, they become motivated to continue to push themselves. They will begin to believe that they can be successful—and you will begin to get the commitment you're seeking.

Set up students so they see incremental progress, too. Some students need feedback daily, while others may be able to go longer periods between feedback sessions. I once worked with a student who needed to see and hear from me on a daily basis, while another student I was mentoring only needed weekly check-ins. Talk with your students to see what they need from you and give them positive reinforcement in a way that is meaningful to them. Find out what they find motivating. I have had students who respond to food as a reinforcement, and others who want one-on-one time. No matter what goal you're working on, motivate your students by offering something you know they will be willing to work for, instead of just guessing what will inspire them.

LEAD**FORWARD**STRATEGY
Build Student Commitment

- **Teach them agency.** Students need to understand how to make choices and decisions that will lead to their growth. Bringing them into a conversation where you discuss their strengths and weaknesses gives them the opportunity to develop an action plan. For example, set up appointments with students who are struggling to make progress. Ask them what support they need. Find out what has *not* happened at school that needs to *start* happening so they feel supported academically, socially, and emotionally. Take the responsibility for their failure away from them and help them develop an action plan for excellence, and you'll show them that you are committed to their success. This will help them commit to their own success, too.

- **Teach them how to develop a plan.** Students need to see excellence in action. When setting goals with students, help them identify realistic actions that will achieve their goals. Some students tend to set lofty goals without acquiring the necessary skills to achieve those goals. For example, if a student who has struggled to pass their classes sets a goal to get all A's on the next grading cycle, but does not currently have the necessary work ethic to achieve this goal, then chances are they will not be successful. Help students set realistic goals and identify two to three action steps that will guide them toward making progress on the goals.

  Remind students that you are looking for progress, not perfection. When you check in with them, talk with them about their actions, not their end goals. Incremental check-ins will help students see that being intentional will help them ultimately reach their goals. Teach them that to *Be Excellent on Purpose* involves intentionality toward a well-defined goal. Through reflection, students will be able to focus on how their actions contribute to their progress. The following questions are suggestions to help students get started in this work:

  - What did I do this week that helped me make progress toward my goals? Why was this helpful?

  - What do I need to stop doing so that I can reach my goals?

  - How have my actions hurt or helped me make progress toward my goals?

  - What were my wins this week? Why?

Build in time for personal reflection and processing. Giving students time to write is the first step. Allow them time to process their thinking with you so you can help them adjust their plan.

Make Them Believe

When students experience success, they begin to hunger for more. However, have you ever looked at a student and seen something in them that they are not able to see in themselves? How do you mold someone into something they don't want to be or don't believe they could be? Some students have been in environments where they have been pitied more than they have been pushed, and don't have the necessary skills for persevering through challenges and hardships. Perhaps they have attended schools that were more focused on blessing their hearts instead of paving a path to excellence. Sometimes we have to believe in our students more than they believe in themselves. Our students come to school with baggage that they cannot check at the door. For some, just coming to school means overcoming an obstacle. Let's reflect on our beliefs about our students and develop a mindset that says the students under our leadership will be successful—even before they believe it themselves.

And I'm not just talking about grades. I'm talking about life. We need to pump so many messages of persistence, perseverance, and positivity into their lives that no matter what choices they make, they will always know they can mentally come back to home base and the messages they heard from us. George Couros, education leader and author of *The Innovator's Mindset*, says it best: "We need to make the positive so loud that the negative becomes impossible to hear." If our students don't have that excitement about themselves, they should get it from us. All students have a story. They need to understand that their current situation is just the beginning. And yes, some students are dealt a bad deck of cards, but we need to teach them how to persevere and find options to improve their circumstances.

I have several amazing teachers in my school, but one in particular is known for his ability to motivate the unmotivated student. Mr. Sierra is an eighth-grade math teacher. He works with students who have significant deficiencies in math. Most of his students have a negative attitude toward math because they have never been successful in the subject. One of Mr. Sierra's students had never passed the math portion of the state test, yet the state of Texas requires eighth-grade students to pass the math assessment as one criterion to enter the ninth grade. When we received the scores, we noticed that 80 percent of Mr. Sierra's students passed the test on the first attempt (including that student who had never passed a math portion of the state test). These were students who had not been successful on this test since they began testing in third grade. A counselor was talking with one of the students about her progress and the student told her, "I didn't think I was going to pass because I never have before, but Mr. Sierra kept telling me I was going to, so I did!"

This is a perfect example of how what we say to our students impacts their mindset. Believing in them, even when they don't believe in themselves, drives us to do whatever is necessary to help them succeed. In addition, when students are taught to set goals and track their progress, they can see the role their choices play in their success. Mr. Sierra told me that he sees his students as scholars, and treats them as such. He is relentless with the positive messages he feeds them, and consistently sets and tracks goals with them. When students begin to see incremental progress, they begin to believe and want to try even harder.

LEAD**FORWARD**STRATEGY
Will Them to Success

- **Recognize the power of your role.** Relationship-building must come before content-giving. You must believe that you are the number-one determinant to the success or failure of your students. If you can't say that phrase without adding a "Yes, but," then you don't believe in the power of your role. External factors will be out of your control, but you cannot let that stop you from focusing on what is *in* your control.

  In order to do this work, we must self-reflect daily. We need to assess where we are and what we have been able to accomplish, and adjust to target areas that will move us to where we desire to be. Continuous improvement for ourselves as educators equates to continuous improvement for our students. We must stay fully charged and committed to the work if we plan to make a difference.

  Once you identify your students' needs, reach out to your extended connections for ideas and strategies that will help you reach your students. Using your relationships with other educators as a catalyst for your personal and professional growth is what makes those relationships powerful. Share your expectations with students and then give them challenging, relevant tasks that will allow them to meet your expectations. Once you have developed a relationship with a student, they want to do whatever they can to meet your expectations. Making a difference means inspiring students to do more—to be more. It is important to be enthusiastic and passionate about your content, but it is even more important to be excited about your students.

- **Advocate for students.** I would argue that most students who are not doing well in school started with a "How to Be Unsuccessful in School" game plan. Do we really think that students wake up and say, "My goal is to fail over and over again in school?" But this can become a pattern for many students if they don't have adults advocating on their behalf. We must not let our students fail! It is imperative that we remove obstacles and barriers so it is impossible for them to fail. I know many believe that this takes extra work and effort on the educator's part, but if we say things like, "All kids can learn," does that mean that they can learn only if they *want* to? When I see that phrase, I understand it as, "All kids can learn if I do what is necessary to make them learn."

  When you notice the same students failing over and over again, the question should be, "What are we doing that is preventing this student from being successful?" Instead of putting all the blame on the backs of students, we need to shoulder a great deal of that responsibility. Don't get me wrong—they do play a role—but sometimes we have to assume some of their responsibilities until we are able to teach them how to understand their role.

  Be diligent in creating systems of support for students. Set up a mentoring program so that students have a person to check in with them while at school. Be a role model for your students. Let them see you as an example of what they can become by sharing your journey to help them create a pathway of their own. Education keynote speaker Angela Maiers says, "Students need role models who are bold, brave, and who embrace vulnerability. Be that for them." Create a safe space for students by being a listening ear and resisting the urge to judge them or their life experiences. Don't try to project your values and norms onto students. Allow them to be who they are and help them make decisions about who they are striving to become and what they want to achieve.

Lastly, use your voice to advocate for your students. If you see a barrier in their life that is within your control or influence to move, speak out about it. Think outside the box and consider different strategies and resources that will help you help your students grow in these areas.

MOVING**FORWARD**

Students need to believe that someone cares about their success and is dedicated and committed to helping them be successful. Identify the barriers to student success and give students the tools to overcome those barriers at school. We cannot control all of the external obstacles that students face outside of school, but there are a number of things we can do during the school day to meet their needs. The atmosphere we create for our students matters. If your students do not have a voice in what is happening in your school or classroom, then the focus is not on the right group. What is best for students may not be what is comfortable or preferred by the adults. Let's remember who we are serving and create an environment that meets the needs of every *student* rather than the adults in the room.

CHAPTER 9
LEAD**FORWARD**JOURNAL

Amplifying student voice

Ways that student voices are amplified in my classroom or school include ...

_____

_____

_____

_____

_____

_____

_____

_____

When working with students who are not motivated to learn what I am teaching, I will adjust my approach to meeting their needs by ...

_____

_____

_____

_____

_____

_____

_____

_____

The most important steps I need to take when setting goals with students include ...

_____

_____

_____

_____

_____

_____

_____

_____

_____

_____

_____

_____

Share your journal entries and ideas at #LeadForward on Twitter.

Become Self-Aware

Knowing others is intelligence; knowing yourself is true wisdom.
Mastering others is strength; mastering yourself is true power.
— LAO-TZU, CHINESE TAOIST PHILOSOPHER

Becoming Self-Aware

IN 2016, ANGELA Maiers, speaker and founder of Choose2Matter, gave the closing keynote at the What Great Educators Do Differently conference in Katy, Texas. Her keynote struck a chord with me, and specifically the ideas she shared about habitudes, which included:

Your Habits + Your Attitude = Who You Are (Habitudes)

We learn who we are when we practice self-awareness, which, according to Maiers, means knowing who you are, refining who you are, and becoming what you are meant to be. This message was timely. Just a few months after hearing this keynote, I would encounter leadership challenges that would test my belief in myself, dim my passion, and cause me to consider leaving the principal seat altogether.

The transition from my first principalship to the second was not as smooth as I expected. I underestimated the amount of change

I needed to make in order to lead, and the level of dedication and commitment required of both me and my staff. We needed to develop systems and structures to move the school forward. Clearly, I couldn't take the same strategies, systems, and structures that were successful at another school and apply them to my new setting. I was not only going to have to lead change, but I was also going to have to change as a leader. My leadership style needed to adapt to meet the needs of my new setting.

Looking back at Maiers' definition of self-awareness, I realized I would have to refine who I was as a leader so I could go through the transformation of becoming what I was meant to be in my new role. Thinking I had leadership figured out was an error on my part.

The truth is, we must be committed to growing and learning—as I covered in the first chapter. If you are not evolving as a leader, you are not growing. If you are still the same leader year after year, you need to take a moment and ask yourself the following question: "How can you ask others to change and grow when you haven't grown or changed yourself?" Although it is difficult to go through transformational change, remember that every challenge is a setup to learn something new. Our experiences are part of the preparation for something we will encounter in the future. The refinement phase of self-awareness can only occur as a result of overcoming challenges and obstacles.

Leadership, specifically the role of the principal, is a position with a small margin of error. The principal's influence can be powerful, but it does not come without a burden. It is a position that requires you to use a range of skills all at the same time to attack a multitude of problems. While fulfilling the role and responsibilities that come with leading students and staff, as well as working with parents and community members, school leaders have to deal with people analyzing and critiquing every decision they make. Outside of your presence, people participate in hypercritical conversations about you as a leader, and when you are around, they say things are going well and sing your praises. This makes trusting others a challenge. This is why it is important to know who you are and what you stand for as a leader. As you start your journey toward self-awareness, consider the following questions:

- Do you know what keeps you going?
- What motivates you?
- Do you know and accept your limitations?
- How do you know when you are acting outside of your integrity?
- Do you know how you are perceived by others?
- Do you know how to bounce back from failure?
- How do you separate truth from opinion?

Remember the list of values you made in Chapter 1? Refer back to it now to help you with these questions. Practicing self-awareness and being in tune with your emotional intelligence are critical skills for successful leaders. If you don't take the time to learn and understand yourself, how can you lead others?

When we know who we are as leaders, on the other hand, we can stand firm in the decisions we make despite what others think we should have done. We develop thicker skin as a result of getting scars along the way. Trust yourself and have the courage to lead despite what the naysayers may say. No matter what you do, someone will always think they can do it better. That is the nature of the business. If you're in a leadership position, people watch everything you do and hang on every word you say, so it is imperative to be mindful of the verbal and nonverbal messages you send. Surround yourself with people who can help to shape your perspective and keep your emotions in check. Remember, you are in charge of yourself. When you lose that focus, you are in great danger of losing your influence as a leader.

LEAD**FORWARD**STRATEGY
Live in Constant Revision

- **Learn from failure.** Spend time reflecting on your journey as a leader. It is so powerful to revisit previous thoughts and experiences that have shaped who you are. Learning how to become better versions of ourselves helps us to adapt to new situations. Owning your failure is the first step toward learning from it. I have often heard that if you are not failing, then you are not growing. How will we know what works if we don't risk trying something new?

  Failure gives you the chance to learn about the situation and yourself. It is your attitude, more than your skill set, that determines how you respond to failure. Be confident in your decision-making and be ready to learn. If you are working to *Be Excellent on Purpose*, you are bound to fail. Remember, it does not define you. It is how you respond to the failure that people will remember the most.

  Journaling is a valuable way to record your successes and failures. It provides a safe space for you to explore your feelings and uncover the constraints or catalysts for your success. Remember that being excellent on purpose means intentionally engaging in practices that promote vulnerability and reflection. Nothing will put you in a more vulnerable state than seeing your thoughts on paper. When you journal, you are identifying private victories and celebrating your success. The mind believes what it sees, so seeing where you are winning and where you need to adjust helps you learn from your failure. By giving your mind the time to process, you clarify your life's purpose and mission. In your journal, you are authoring your life in real time, which allows you to make impactful decisions that will make a difference.

By giving your mind the time to process, you clarify your life's purpose and mission.

- **Practice gratitude.** Being chosen to lead students, staff, and a community is not something to take lightly. We were chosen for this role for a reason. So much of what we do, and what we fail to do, for that matter, determines the success, or lack thereof, of our students and staff. Instead of focusing on all the daily tasks that must get done every day, let's shift our attitude so we feel grateful for the opportunity to serve each day. Let's face it: We asked for these positions. And yes, while at times it can be overwhelming, we still occupy the seat that so many deeply desire to obtain. Leading is not for the faint of heart, and although many desire it, few are chosen.

  Take a moment and record your thoughts of gratitude. You could write down at least one thing you are grateful for each day. This practice encourages you to think of something positive that has impacted your life. Writing down moments of gratitude in a journal gives you a space to keep track of the moments in your life that matter the most. Selecting one thing requires you to identify something significant. This goes beyond completing the journal in a perfunctory matter just to check it off your list.

  You don't need to list the obvious things; you know that you are grateful for your family, friends, and material possessions. Think beyond that context. Here is an example: "I am grateful for the interaction that I had with a student today. Even though it started off negatively, I was able to practice my relationship-building skills, which transformed the interaction."

Seek to find slices of gratitude in the challenges and obstacles you face. This will help you focus on growth opportunities instead of setbacks. When you reframe your thinking in this way, you will find the good in any situation. Another idea is to engage in moments of mindfulness. This allows your brain to slow down so you can refocus on many areas of your life. Practice a kind act. Doing something for someone else not only makes them feel valued and appreciated, but it also makes you feel good because you were able to help someone. Challenge yourself and others to follow *The No Complaining Rule*, which is outlined in Jon Gordon's book of the same name. This challenge will focus your time and energy on solutions instead of problems.

How you choose to practice gratitude is up to you. Just be grateful for the journey and never underestimate your influence as a leader. A leader who practices gratitude and positivity will benefit from a massive return on that investment.

- **Leave it better than you found it.** Take time to focus on your leadership accomplishments, both individually and collectively. Look for an indelible mark of your leadership on the lives of the students and staff you serve, and if it's hard to find, then what is the purpose of your journey?

  Walk through your school and ask yourself if your school visually represents who you are and what you are about as a leader. Listen to the conversation. Do your students and staff sound like you? Your school is a reflection of your leadership. If you don't like what is reflected, it is your responsibility to address it. For example, at one point in my leadership career, I discovered that my philosophical beliefs were not aligned with what was happening in the school. I was disappointed because I realized my perception was different from reality, and the reality was negatively impacting my school culture. While this was difficult to accept, I knew that I could not ignore what I'd discovered.

The first step in addressing the issue was to talk with teachers to identify trends. Then I shared my findings with my staff. I owned the problem. Even though the solution would involve more than just me as the leader, I took responsibility for the current state of affairs. Teachers volunteered to participate in a focus group meeting with me, and getting their insight helped me identify strategies for solving the problems we were facing. When you are faced with a situation that needs to be corrected, I encourage you to also own up to the problem, and ask others to help you with the solution.

Just as you involve students in the process of setting goals, involve others in the work of making your vision a reality. It gives them the opportunity to be part of the legacy.

Leading Through Crisis

In 2016, within weeks of each other, two students from my school, a first-grader and a fifth-grader, died in unrelated incidents. I hadn't learned anything in "principal school" that prepared me to lead my staff through such a difficult time. The death of two children shook me to the core as a mother and as a school leader. Not knowing how to process these tragedies, being unsure about how to deliver the news to my staff, and the hardest thing of all, preparing for conversations with the parents of those students, made me feel unsettled.

In times of crisis, everyone looks to the leader, but who does the leader look to for support and guidance? We must feel our way through certain situations. Saying that I didn't know what to say was actually more comforting to my staff and parents than trying to pull words together for the sake of saying something. Silence and tears speak volumes when others are hurting. Sometimes just speaking for the sake of speaking blocks our ability to feel our way through the tragedy.

Just six months after the death of two students, I had to lead a different staff through the unexpected death of a colleague.

Internal factors are not the only crisis situations that leaders must face. This became apparent after Hurricane Harvey devastated the Houston metropolitan area and Southeast Texas, dumping sixty inches of rain, which led to extreme flooding. Some staff members and students at my school lost their homes, while others were displaced for months. Coming back to school eleven days after the storm to face my faculty, who had more pressing things on their minds than getting back to our core business, was a daunting task. We started a new school year just a week before the storm, and now, just weeks later, we were going to restart the school year after living through the physical destruction and emotional turmoil that accompanies a natural disaster. There were no words that I could say to ease the transition into life after Harvey.

After reflecting on a year and a half of emotional turmoil, though, I realized that I was so focused on leading others that I had not taken the time to take care of myself. It reminded me of the instructions you hear on the airplane before takeoff regarding the use of oxygen masks: Be sure to adjust and secure your mask before helping others.

Leading a school through a crisis requires leaders to use skills that are not necessarily connected to teaching and learning. Recognizing that school leaders are not just leaders of the day-to-day functions at school, but also leaders whose staff and community look to for guidance and direction during a time of crisis, will help leaders understand the significant role they play. There isn't a playbook for every crisis situation; however, I'll share four pieces of advice summarized from David Lammy, a member of British Parliament.[4] Here's a summary of his four practical ways to lead through a crisis:

1. Trust your instincts. Crisis situations are unique events that are never the same. When you first encounter a crisis, you can expect to feel a range of emotions, including anxiety over how to lead others through the situation. In most cases, you probably have knowledge about how to address the situation or you know someone you can call for help. However, in new situations, your scope of knowledge may be limited and you may not have another person you can reach out to who has had a similar experience. Trust your instincts. Think about how you would want to be led through this situation. Lead with service. You can never go wrong by showing compassion and acts of kindness to others during a crisis situation.

2. Stay calm. During a crisis, people will ask many questions and demonstrate a range of emotions. The leader should offer a sense of calm. Your emotions and internal thoughts may be all over the place, but hold yourself together rather than displaying them in front of your staff. Your calmness helps to settle the atmosphere. Staying calm does not mean you can't show emotion. It means using your emotions productively so you can help others move beyond the crisis to healing.

3. Communicate the facts. Gather the facts and only communicate what you know to be true. There may be some information that you cannot share publicly. Share what you can and remember that the goal of communicating the facts is to reassure your team and community, and share the plan for moving forward. A number of spin-off stories are often developed during a crisis situation, so stating only the facts helps to communicate the right story. It is okay if you need to script yourself to help make sure your thoughts are well-developed, and that you're expressing only the key points of your message.

4. Support your people. During a crisis, people look to leaders for answers, guidance, and resolution. Understand that successfully leading through a crisis creates trust and forms a bond between you and your team. Lead with your heart and to the best of your ability, and seek to meet the needs of others. This could mean gathering resources, both human and fiscal, and taking the time to meet physical and emotional needs. Use your leadership influence to leverage resources to support your team or community through a crisis.

In addition to caring for others during a crisis, remember to care for yourself. Never underestimate the emotional toll that crisis situations may have on you as a leader. On top of dealing with the crisis like everyone else, you have the additional emotional toll of having other people relying on you. To me, that's the exhausting part of being a leader—having to spend pieces of myself to take care of others when I'm already feeling depleted. The moment you take a break from leading, be prepared for a range of emotions to come flooding in. You cannot control the crisis, but you can control how you respond. Take time for yourself so that you have the clarity and perspective you need to lead others.

LEAD**FORWARD**STRATEGY
Practice Self-Care

- **Take physical and emotional inventory.** As the saying goes, "If your cup is empty, you can't pour into others." Leadership can be emotionally draining. On certain days, everyone takes what they need from you, leaving you with nothing for yourself. Leadership requires you to give, but you can't give more than you have. There's no emotional loan department that you can borrow from. Unless, of course, you give to the point where you become physically ill. And this happens more often than it should.

In order to effectively lead others, you must continue to fill your cup each day. Recognize when you are becoming emotionally and physically tapped out, and stop before you are completely empty. You will be of no use to yourself or others if you do not practice self-care. What do you need to tweak so you are the best version of yourself? During a crisis, give yourself time to process your emotions. Your job is not to be everything to all people. Your job is to be a steady calm and a safe space for those you are leading.

- **Phone a friend.** Do you know leaders who try to figure out how to solve every challenge that comes across their desk? This approach can be isolating, and it limits ideas and potential solutions. You will always be faced with something new that you have never faced before. Instead of trying to figure it out alone, call another leader to help you process it. You can't handle all crisis situations in the same way, but it is best to have a frame of reference as a starting point. If you still think you can lead without the help of others, you are giving yourself more credit than you should. Ask for help and be comfortable in not knowing how to do everything.

- **Take time off.** The initial crisis situation is temporary; it is the aftermath of the crisis that lingers. Know when to take a day off to disconnect from work so that you can reconnect with yourself. If you can't miss a day of work to pull yourself together, then you have more leadership problems than you think. Take breaks during the day to check in with yourself. Spend time collecting your thoughts and recharging emotionally. Leave the building to get a coffee or lunch. It is okay to take a break. Your leadership strength comes from being self-aware and taking care of yourself so you are able to properly care for others.

Managing Your Productivity

As a leader, is it possible to do everything you need to do at work during the workday so that you can have a life away from school? The answer is yes! First, remember that the work will never be complete. There are peak seasons that may require you to come in early or stay late, but this should not be your norm. Working in this manner leads to burnout. In a blog post by Dr. Adam Fraser titled, "It's a Lonely Job: How Can We Help Stressed-out Principals?" he shares that workplace demands, high levels of burnout, stress, difficulty sleeping, and depressive symptoms are issues principals are dealing with at a range of 1.3 to 2.2 times higher than the population. Although the study he references was conducted in Australia, it has relevance to principals everywhere.

Baruti Kafele, an education speaker and author, shared his experience of principal burnout in an article written for the July 2018 edition of *Educational Leadership*. He specifically talked about his "career-questioning moment." In his article, Kafele urges leaders to go back to their why when they are going through a rough patch. I couldn't agree more. As mentioned in Chapter 1, identifying your why is the first step to *Be Excellent on Purpose*. It's also the most critical step to staying on that path. But it's not the *only* step. After you refocus on the work and center on your why, you're ready to develop a plan for how you will manage the daily load. There is no perfect plan for how to manage yourself and all the tasks you must complete, but not having a plan will lead to failure.

I once met someone at a conference who told me she felt

ineffective, like she was working outside of her leadership purpose. She was spending most of her time putting out fires and managing the problems of others, and lacked the time and energy to work on the important task of leading. Can you relate? Taking care of yourself also means giving yourself time to keep growing, rather than forcing yourself into a rut where all you do is take care of other people. As we began to talk through specific examples, which included managing adult behavior, dealing with difficult parents, meeting central office demands, and ensuring that students are achieving at high levels, she realized that she didn't have a daily plan that allowed her to focus and ultimately reach her leadership goals.

Planning for excellence is the only way to achieve excellent results. Those who plan and execute their plan make it look easy because intentional effort on the front end leads to exceptional results. Before I learned how to do that, everything I was working on was due at the same time, and I wasn't able to get anything done in an efficient or productive manner. It became frustrating and overwhelming, and I knew I needed to figure out how to maximize my time during the day. I couldn't keep working until all hours of the night! Something had to change.

When work is taking over your family and personal wellness time, you are on a dangerous path. But you have control over how you spend your time and energy on a daily basis. While you will get hit by a heavy workload at times, and you must put in more hours to get certain projects done, step back and determine if this is your usual mode or an occasional scenario. If it happens all too often, you need to create a plan for maximizing your time and getting things done in the most efficient manner possible.

Once you find a system that works for you, expect to be tempted to fall back into your old routine. Remember the backwards bicycle story and how old habits die hard? The longer you have been doing something, the harder it is to break that habit, especially when you are trying something new and you feel pressure, or a hard deadline is approaching. Give yourself grace as you form new habits that will help you increase your productivity. Start somewhere, and start now.

LEAD**FORWARD**STRATEGY
Plan to Be Productive

- **Check in with yourself before starting your workday.** Starting the day running at full speed is equivalent to sprinting the first leg of a marathon. You may get things done quickly, but you'll run right through your stamina and burn out. When you enter your office, if possible, enter where you have the least amount of interaction. This will allow you to get settled in before you begin tackling the day. Engage in at least ten minutes of quiet time. Use the time to read, meditate, listen to calming music, engage in a Bible study, or do anything else that helps you feel centered. This may seem unproductive, but you are actually preparing to be more productive and self-aware when you take this time to focus on yourself and set the tone for the day. Besides, this is probably the only quiet time you will get. If this is a challenge at school, do it at home right after you wake up.

- **Plan the day with intention.** Productivity increased for me when I began planning all of my tasks, including when I arrived at work, when I ate lunch, and when I closed down for the day. If you need to plan restroom breaks, you are almost at the point of no return! Being intentional with my time helped me to make sure that I was giving all my tasks the proper amount of attention. During our morning meeting, my assistant and I review tasks that need to be completed during the day, week, or month. We give each task a title and a time frame. For example, we need to complete the semester data review report in the next two weeks, and we need to allot two hours to complete this task. My assistant adds it to my calendar and there are no double-bookings. Everything is scheduled and put in a folder until it is time to work on it.

Before this process, I started out on the wrong foot because I was keeping stacks of paper in my office and working on tasks as I felt compelled to handle them. It was the way I'd done things for most of my administrative career. I shuffled through the same stacks every day, and although everything got done, it was as if I was always working against the clock to complete tasks instead of intentionally planning time for when I would do them. Now, at the end of each day, I print the calendar for the next day, and after my morning quiet time, I review the calendar and prepare for my day. This has increased my productivity tremendously because I have the outcomes in front of me and a specific plan for achieving them.

- **Be present and visible.** I prefer to be outside of my office during the day, but let's be realistic: Some things must be done in the principal's office. Do not feel guilty about staying in the office to complete your work. Schedule your office days and communicate with your staff so they know where you are if you are not visible. It is unrealistic to think that spending all of your time in classrooms and being out and about in the building is the best way to work. It is not. You must have scheduled office time to get your tasks done.

  The same is true for coaching days. Coaching days are spent in hallways and classrooms, coaching and building relationships with teachers and students. I schedule this time at least three days a week. If I can't manage full days because I have scheduling conflicts, I schedule half-days. I can complete some office tasks while I am in the building coaching, so I pack those in my backpack along with snacks and water. Coaching means being present in the hallways and visiting classrooms to engage in the learning with students. I give instructional feedback and review how the systems and structures are working. Being more present and visible on those days decreases the number of concerns, questions, and problems that seem to make it to my office, which increases my productivity even more.

MOVING**FORWARD**

No one ever said this journey would be easy, and not all people are cut out for this level of leadership. But we need to work on ourselves, our productivity, and our mental well-being if we're going to leave a lasting legacy as leaders. Find others who understand and appreciate the journey, and pull them into your network for continued learning and growth. Leadership is an evolving position, and each situation should help you grow into a better version of yourself. Think of the challenges you face as lessons designed to help you learn and refine your skills as a leader. If you are the same leader that you were the year before, and have absolutely no desire to get better, then please move out of the way so someone else who is on fire for leadership can lead. Respect the role, understand the position, stay committed to growth, and keep the leadership torch burning.

CHAPTER 9
LEADFORWARDJOURNAL

Practice being self-aware

I am a better leader because I experienced failure in this area ...

_____

_____

_____

_____

_____

_____

This failure helped me to strengthen my skills as a leader by ...

_____

_____

_____

_____

_____

In order to care for others, my plan for practicing self-care will be ...

_____

_____

_____

_____

_____

By intentionally mapping out my day, the following tasks have the highest priority ...

_____

_____

_____

_____

_____

In order to ensure that I protect time to accomplish priority tasks, I will ...

_____

_____

_____

_____

_____

Strategies I will use to increase my daily productivity include ...

_____

_____

_____

_____

_____

Share your journal entries and ideas at #LeadForward on Twitter.

Create Stories Worth Telling

The best leaders are storytellers. Just as the leader sets the pace, the leader starts the story. The adoption and appreciation for story starts at the top.
— KINDRA HALL, PRESIDENT AND CHIEF STORYTELLING OFFICER AT STELLER COLLECTIVE

Tell Your School's Story

I USED TO SAY that I had no desire to move into a leadership position beyond the campus level. I felt that higher-level positions were steeped in politics and more focused on political moves and power plays. But the more I thought about the influence a campus leader has, the more I realized that my perception was not accurate, and that I *did* participate in politics to impact legislation that could create a positive impact on our campus.

Wise leaders often use stories as a channel of influence, whether or not they are in political situations. Stories serve to inspire and motivate their staff, students, and community members. As the storyteller in chief, telling stories gives you the opportunity to communicate your vision, values, and mission. You have the chance to appeal to emotions, and to tell stories that reflect what the organization is trying to achieve. If you develop, practice, and frequently utilize the skill of storytelling, it will serve you well.

According to Kindra Hall, chief storytelling officer of Steller Collective, if you want to make sure people listen when you speak, tell stories that illustrate the value of your message. During a visit to the Texas State Capitol building in Austin, my fellow colleagues and I decided to visit with the legislative director of the senator who represents our school district. First, we told the legislative director what district and school we represented. When I shared my district and school, she chimed in immediately, "My parents live near there." When my colleague mentioned where she was currently serving as the principal, and that she had previously served as the principal in the neighborhood school where the legislative director grew up, the director put her hand on her heart and said, "That was my elementary school!"

I could tell that she had positive memories from elementary school and could probably tell stories about how it impacted her life. I told the legislative director that the reaction she had when she thought about her experience in school was the reason we came to Austin to discuss the future of public education in Texas. She may not remember the names or even the points the group made, but she will remember the experience she had with the principal from the school she once attended. What started as a visit to talk about critical issues in Texas public education turned into a conversation about what we can do to make school memorable for students in Texas. The story changed the conversation.

Marshall Ganz, author and lecturer at Harvard University, shared his thoughts on recapturing the narrative and the art of storytelling in a 2009 article written for *Sojourners Magazine*. In "Why Stories Matter," Ganz discusses three steps to telling a powerful story:

1. Story of Self. As a leader, people want to know what inspires and fuels your passion to lead. They want to know why you have been called to lead, and what purpose drives your passion. You are the author of your story and if you don't control your own narrative, someone else will.

During my first principalship, I was excited and eager to be given the opportunity to lead. As eager as I was, I could tell that some staff members were scared to death. I didn't understand why at the time, but later realized that I didn't take the time to get to know the staff and allow them to get to know *me*. At that time, my concern for the work was greater than my concern for the workers. I knew myself, but I did not take into account the fact that the staff didn't know me or what I was about as a leader. Oh, they knew my professional background because they Googled me and asked around before I got there. They knew general information about my family, specifically that I was married and had two children, but they didn't know my *why*. They had no idea what drove me as a leader. Once I shared my personal story and told them about the values that drove me as a leader, real transformation began to happen.

2. Story of Us. The story of us allows us to find our common purpose and figure out where our lives intersect to bring us to the point of where we are today. It allows us to focus on how we ended up in this space at this time. The story of us helps people to see each other's similarities and differences. Through that sharing of our stories, we begin to learn and respect the journey of others, and build relationships.

3. Story of Now. The story of now helps organizations define who they are and what they want to achieve together. During this phase, we must build a sense of urgency around achieving the goals of the group. The story of now is where organizations see their current reality versus where they want to be, and begin to transform hope into action. The stories you tell must compel others to want to keep pushing forward so they can create the next story. Help your organization focus on the inputs of the vision rather than the final output. Think about the actions you take every day to reflect the brand. This is where the magic happens, and it's how you reach the ultimate goal.

LEAD**FORWARD**STRATEGY
Become the Chief Storyteller

- **Identify and live your school's brand.** When someone says the name of your school, do people listening know what your school stands for? If we think about some of the most popular brands, we see that the logo or slogan represents what the brand is about. Be sure that your brand promise does the same thing for your school. Think about what you want to associate with your organization, and develop a tagline that speaks to that. This is the tagline you will share with others as a quick and easy description of your school's purpose.

  For example, I wanted my current campus to be known for striving for excellence, so my personal tagline, *Be Excellent on Purpose*, became the tagline for our school.

  Be sure that what you say matches what you are demonstrating every day. For example, if those outside of my school were to encounter a member of my team who did not represent our school's brand of excellence, it would diminish the power of our brand. Make sure that everyone in your school knows your brand and understands that they should be communicating—and demonstrating—it to others. Then communicate your brand in as many ways as possible. Use social media, word of mouth, visuals, and swag.

- **Develop an elevator speech about your school.** If you were on an elevator for thirty to sixty seconds and someone asks you what makes your school great, what would you say? Your elevator speech should make people want to come for a visit. It should paint a picture of the experiences that students and staff have on a daily basis. Consider the following questions:

- What benefits do your students receive as a result of coming to your school?

- What are some distinguishing facts about your school that make it unique?

- How does your school enhance the educational experience of the students it serves?

If your elevator pitch is true and memorable, it will become the story that people tell about your school. It will become the representation of your brand. Hook the listener so they want to experience your school, and when they arrive, show them that you put your mission into action as well as into words.

What are you doing to share the greatness of your school? How do you share the message with others to amplify your story?

Joe Sanfelippo, the superintendent of Fall Creek School District in Fall Creek, Wisconsin, does this better than any leader I know. I have never been to Fall Creek, Wisconsin; in fact, I had never even heard of it until I began hearing Joe talk about the great work they did there. He showed images and videos to accompany his words, and these strategies helped me create a picture of what students and staff were experiencing at Fall Creek. At a conference, Joe was passing out Fall Creek T-shirts and other swag. He asked those who got a T-shirt to post an image on social media of us wearing our shirts. I was amazed at how many people from all over the country owned Fall Creek gear. The story of Fall Creek was being shared by people who had never stepped one foot in the school district.

What are you doing to share the greatness of your school? How do you share the message with others to amplify your story? Plan and practice your speech so that you are ready to share it. Your elevator speech may be the only opportunity you have to share about your school, so make it exceptional.

- **Organize your story.** To become a storyteller, craft your stories in a way that grabs attention by increasing empathy and emotion. Every educator has a number of stories waiting to be told. What are yours? Make sure that when you tell stories, you're projecting the messages that you want to share. Demonstrate what you're doing in a positive light, and show the world how important education is to the future of society. To do that, make sure your stories are well-organized.

  Discuss the struggles and successes of your organization, and the obstacles you've personally overcome. Give specific details that help the listener connect to the story in a meaningful way. The goal is for the listener to become a part of the journey through the glimpses you give them. Find a pattern that works for the structure of your story, and then begin crafting stories that paint vivid images of the work people are doing inside your organization. Once you find a format that works, use it again and again to give your stories consistency!

Protect the Story

"We must protect this house," an Under Armour advertising campaign told us back in 2003. This saying makes me think of an organization with people coming together to work toward a vision. In order to move the organization forward, all stakeholders, which includes staff, students, parents, and community members, must know the vision and their role in communicating it to others. Keeping the vision, mission, and values at the center of the work helps keep members of the organization informed and on track. Unfortunately, the vision can be derailed by things that are outside of our control.

How do you create storytellers inside and outside of your organization, and teach them how to tell the story of your school or district? What are you doing to protect your house, which includes the people and the work? Being the chief storyteller doesn't mean that you are the only one controlling the narrative. It means that you are telling the story in a way that inspires others to not only share the story, but also be participants in the story's creation. When you have an entire team of people telling your story, you have an entire team of people protecting your house and *controlling* the story.

We all make mistakes. Unfortunately, people often amplify mistakes made by educators. It is common for leaders to take the heat when something goes wrong in their school. Our society imposes a small margin for error, which creates a tremendous amount of pressure on school leaders. People expect schools to get things right at all times, which is unrealistic. Then, instead of working together to resolve concerns, people start speaking to the wrong audience, which leads to unproductive storytelling.

Twice, I have experienced being the center of someone's social media rant. In both cases, the stories were not accurate. In fact, they were so embellished that I thought I had blacked out and missed most of the event! The misinformation was running wild and I needed to get in front of it to get the correct information to my community. When things like this happen, it is so hard not to take the attacks personally. I felt like I had let my community down. However, this was where my work in the community proved valuable. Many leaders think that one mistake will destroy the confidence the community has in their leadership. This may be true if your community doesn't know what you are about, what you are trying to achieve, or how they are part of the work. When you include your community as a shared stakeholder in the story, you build an environment where they feel compelled to advocate and protect your story because they feel connected to you and the school. They become part of your team, and they want to protect your house.

Unfortunately, there will always be naysayers who question your ability to lead. That is part of being a leader. Not everyone will support or be happy with your decisions, but those who want you to be successful because your success is a win for them, the students, and the school will help you through the challenging times if you have built those relationships. Brené Brown, author and keynote speaker, talks about the critics in the arena of life. In her work, she uses the words of Theodore Roosevelt to make the point that critics may have loud voices and large audiences, but those loud voices and audiences will be minimized by those who support you.

When faced with challenges and negative attacks on you or your school story, stay in front of the issue. Transparency is key. When we mess up, we must own it, correct it, and move forward. Be courageous and address the elephant in the room. If people don't know you and what you are about as a leader, they can't support you or your school. Be transparent and honest. People can forgive mistakes when they feel they are coming from an honest place.

LEAD**FORWARD**STRATEGY
Build Your Story on Relationships

- **Connect with families.** One of the most important roles of a school leader is to connect and engage with families. In order to cultivate relationships with your families, be visible and approachable. Make yourself known to your community so they get to know you and what you stand for as a leader. Attend extracurricular activities so you can meet parents. Be sure you are visible in high-traffic areas during arrival and dismissal. This allows parents to see your presence on a regular basis, which makes you accessible to them. Get to know your parents by name and make every effort to address them when you have the opportunity. Make each family feel important. When you create this personal connection, your families will begin to feel a connection to who you are as a person—and will listen to your storytelling rather than the stories of others.

- **Share the message.** Think of ways you can communicate the work of your school or district to those who are not part of the day-to-day work. Video messages are great and they give the community an opportunity to see and hear you. Communicate through electronic newsletters on a consistent basis to keep the community informed. Using videos and visuals helps people to connect and relate to your story. Find the platforms where your community lives. For example, sharing images on our school Instagram account is a great way to get a message to my students. They live there, but their parents live on Facebook. Another idea is to invite the community into your school and allow them to see the work in action.

Think of ways parents and community members can partner with you to provide students with exceptional experiences. Consider holding a career fair where parents and community members talk about their work and how they impact the community. Invite parents to spend part of the day learning with their child. This will give them the opportunity to see what a typical day is like at school, which gives them a better understanding of how to support their child at home. When you form partnerships, it means all parties have a stake in the school story and a responsibility to share the story with others.

- **Be transparent and always share the truth.** People respect a leader who is authentic and tells the truth, even if they don't agree with the message. People want to know where they stand and how the message will impact them. When facts are kept a secret, it gives everyone the ability to create their own story. Nothing fuels a story more than misinformation and a lack of details. When your parents know who you are as a leader, and the work you are leading at the school, they will speak up to correct any misinformation.

MOVING**FORWARD**

What stories are you creating together with your students, staff, and community? When the story of your school is co-created, it means more. You are living and creating the experience together. When you are telling the story of your school, focus on specifics. Don't leave out things that seem insignificant. What seems small to you may be the missing ingredient for someone else. The amount of energy you put into being the storyteller in chief will determine the amount of energy that is pumped back into your school.

In Chapter 2, I talked about the influence a leader's words have on an organization. Use your words and actions to create your school's story, and then spread that story far and wide. A leader's action or inaction drives an organization's story. What messages are you sending to internal and external stakeholders about your school? Is your tagline or statement of purpose evident in the daily actions and decisions of the school? Messages of excellence are seen and heard. What you do must match what you say if you are to *Be Excellent on Purpose*.

CHAPTER 10
LEAD**FORWARD**JOURNAL

Create stories worth telling

If I only had thirty seconds to tell the story of my organization, what three key aspects would I discuss?

_____

_____

_____

_____

How is the story of my school being told by

- Students?

  _____

  _____

  _____

- Teachers?

  _____

  _____

  _____

- Parents?

  _____

  _____

  _____

- Community Members?

_____

_____

_____

_____

In order to protect the narrative of our organization, I need to ensure that ...

_____

_____

_____

_____

_____

_____

_____

_____

_____

_____

_____

_____

_____

_____

_____

_____

_____

Share your journal entries and ideas at #LeadForward on Twitter.

CONCLUSION

Dare to Be Different

ROWING UP, I can recall kids daring each other to do something out of the ordinary. The ultimate dare was when someone would "double-dog dare" you to do something. The kids who liked challenges and were not afraid to take risks would accept a dare in a heartbeat. The kids who were more reserved would watch what was going to happen from the sidelines.

While this tactic of risk-taking evolves and becomes more sophisticated as we grow older, it makes me wonder where the leaders are who take the double-dog dares. What does a double-dog dare look like in action? The leaders who dare to be different are the ones who constantly disrupt the status quo so that students and teachers continue to grow. There is no ceiling or point of arrival in leadership. Leaders who dare to be different stay committed to continuous growth and achievement. These leaders are driven by purpose and have an unrelenting sense of determination to contribute to a greater good. The work is never finished.

Those who dare to be different are comfortable with others

challenging their thinking. In fact, they welcome the questioning and the challenge because it helps them get better. Leaders who lead boldly choose to be bothered and challenged by what others believe to be impossible. They have big dreams for their schools and the courage to not only pursue those dreams, but the will to do what is necessary to make those dreams a reality. They understand that big things don't happen with small thinking.

In an earlier chapter of the book, I talked about Dr. Max Goodwin, medical director on the NBC show *New Amsterdam*. On episode seventeen of season one, New York City was in the middle of a deadly blizzard. People outside of the hospital who needed medical attention had no way of getting to the hospital because the city was completely shut down. Dr. Goodwin told his team that if patients couldn't get to the hospital, then the hospital would go to them. Teams of two traversed the impassable conditions to render care to patients in immediate need. This approach to providing care was unconventional and extremely dangerous considering the weather conditions the team had to encounter, but it did not stop Dr. Goodwin from taking the risk. Initially, his team was not on board, but Dr. Goodwin didn't let that stop him from putting on his coat and heading out despite his own significant personal health struggles.

Modeling what you want others to do is definitely a positive way to lead for impact. Leaders must be willing to take the first bite out of something new. Don't ask others to do something you are not willing to do as well.

Eventually, the snow caused the hospital to lose power, which put the care of patients in jeopardy. All of the people in the hospital were sent to the only floor that had limited power. While this transition was occurring, one of the patients was in the operating room undergoing emergency open heart surgery and began to lose blood. Without power, the surgery was extremely risky, but without a blood transfusion, there was virtually no hope for survival. Dr. Goodwin asked for volunteers to donate blood, but his initial plea fell on deaf ears. Once he gained the attention of the room, he used the power of story to appeal to the emotions of the large group. He humanized their situation and took the focus off of their needs and put the focus on someone else who had a greater need. Both scenes demonstrated exceptional courage, resolve, and dedication to others.

This demonstration of leadership caused me to reflect on what I am willing to risk to ensure that those I am charged with leading, including myself, are becoming better each day. How are you challenging others to dare to be different? If others are not growing under your leadership, what do you need to do to change your approach? One of the most important parts of leadership is inspiring others to be better, which often means exposing them to new experiences or helping them to achieve things they never thought possible. How are you using words to inspire others? Do you have a process for giving purposeful feedback that helps others grow? Are you able to bring people together around a common purpose and goal? Do you know how to lead difficult conversations and help others engage in productive conflict? How do you amplify student voice on your campus? Are you able to view your campus through an equity lens to ensure that all students feel safe, secure, and supported academically, socially, and emotionally?

A commitment to excellence is what distinguishes great leaders from good ones. Taking your leadership to the next level requires intentional practice, emotional intelligence, and self-awareness. "When you learn better, you do better," are words for leaders to live by while in constant revision. Your growth as a leader is never done. Position yourself so that you are engaging in experiences that are equipping you to inspire and transform. Look for opportunities to improve your leadership craft. Engage in experiences that push you out of your knowledge and comfort zone. Think of the level of training athletes undergo to prepare for athletic performances. Having the mindset of a winner will only take an athlete so far. Expecting to win means nothing unless they are training like a champion.

For every new skill you are working to develop, put in the time to train so that you are operating at your peak when it is time to perform. When it comes to pursuing excellence, the destination is never final. The journey is endless, but the rest stops along the way, which are the moments you celebrate the wins and accomplishments, are priceless. Take the time to reflect on the journey and know that through your reflection you will likely find another path to traverse. As you prepare your gear for another adventure, take all of your learning and experiences with you, and when the journey becomes challenging, remember that the best solution is to *Be Excellent on Purpose.*

Notes

1. "Nikola Tesla described the modern smartphone—in 1926," Big Think, June 12, 2015, https://bigthink.com/words-of-wisdom/nikola-tesla-2.

2. "Confronting Implicit Bias Through Exemplary Educator Preparation," National Education Association, Center for Great Public Schools, 2018, https://www.nea.org/assets/docs/23840%20Confronting%20Implicit%20Bias%20Thru%20Exemp%20Teacher%20Prep-v2.pdf.

3. Shane Safir, "5 Keys to Challenging Implicit Bias," Edutopia.org, March 14, 2016. https://www.edutopia.org/blog/keys-to-challenging-implicit-bias-shane-safir.

4. "Leading Through a Crisis," video featuring David Lammy, Harvard Business Review, August 7, 2012, https://hbr.org/video/2226821023001/leading-through-a-crisis.

About the Author

Dr. Sanée Bell is the principal of Morton Ranch Junior High in Katy, Texas. She has served as an administrator at both the elementary and secondary levels since 2005, and also taught middle school and high school English and coached girls basketball. In 2015, the Katy ISD recognized Sanée as the Elementary Principal of the Year. She earned her doctorate degree in Educational Leadership with an emphasis in Curriculum and Instruction from the University of Houston Clear Lake. Sanée is passionate about authentic, purposeful learning for students and teachers, and the impact of leadership on teacher engagement, student learning, and school culture. Follow her online @saneebell.

Acknowledgments

INDIVIDUAL ACCOMPLISHMENTS ARE not possible without the help of a group of people who encourage and support you on the journey. I would not have been able to write this book without being given the opportunity to learn from and lead my students, staff, and multiple communities in the Katy Independent School District.

I would especially like to thank the staff and students of Cimarron Elementary and Morton Ranch Junior High for being committed, excited, and dedicated to the leadership vision I charged us with fulfilling. Thank you for following and supporting me.

I would also like to thank my colleagues and friends who celebrate, promote, and encourage me to share my voice and stories with others. You push me to be vulnerable and to explore new ideas and new ways of thinking. Thank you for the encouraging texts, phone calls, and Voxer messages throughout this process. Those interactions helped me reach the finish line. Thank you, Mark Barnes, for giving me the opportunity to launch this new series. This connection is definitely an example of what it means to use your excellence to connect with others. Carrie White-Parrish, you were my lifeline during the toughest moments of this project. You are truly a blessing and absolutely amazing at what you do! Jennifer Jas, thank you for your extra set of eyes and fine attention to detail. Your finishing touches made all the difference.

I have been truly blessed in my career with talents and skills that have allowed me to impact and inspire others, and I know that all glory and honor belong to God for the blessings that He has afforded to me on my life journey. For all that I have been able to accomplish in my career, nothing would have been possible without the support of my husband. Marvin, thank you for allowing me to learn and share my passion without limits. Thank you for supporting me as I pursue excellence in all that I do and for keeping me lifted in prayer. To Richmond and Paige, thank you for fueling my passion as a leader. I have become a better educator because of each of you. Thank you for supporting my dreams and sharing me with other children. You two are my greatest blessings and the best work I have ever produced.

This book is an example of what it means to set a goal, develop a plan, and put intentional actions in place to make that goal a reality. Remember, you will always have to be better than good just to be considered equal. Never be satisfied with average and always strive to *Be Excellent on Purpose* in ALL aspects of your life.

More from the
LEAD**FORWARD**SERIES

LEADFORWARD
Stories & Strategies for Teacher Leaders

The Lead Forward Series from Times 10 Publications features world-class teacher leaders sharing the stories and strategies that will inspire you to be the best you can be, while always leading forward. Learn more about the series and our team at WeLeadForward.com.

QUIET KIDS COUNT
Unleashing the True Potential of Introverts

By Chrissy Romano Arrabito (@TheConnectedEDU)

The grade level or content you teach doesn't matter; you will have them sitting in your room—the introverts, the quiet kids, and the not-so-quiet, but introverts just the same. They don't cause trouble and, for the most part, they earn good grades. But these are the kids who tend to fade into the background and slip through the cracks. The ones who are so often overlooked, or in some cases, misunderstood.

In Lead Forward Series book number two, Chrissy Romano Arrabito provides a guidebook to help you better understand the nature of *all* types of introverts and to allay the misconceptions about them. She provides useful tips and strategies to help these students reach their full potential. *Quiet Kids Count* is a call to action for educators to step up and meet the needs of ALL learners—not just the ones who command the most attention in our schools.

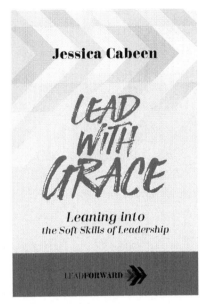

Jessica Cabeen

LEAD
WITH
GRACE

*Leaning into
the Soft Skills of Leadership*

LEADFORWARD »

LEAD WITH GRACE
Leaning Into the Soft Skills of Leadership

*By Jessica Cabeen
(@jessicacabeen)*

With technology, we interact with families, students, and staff 24-7, not just during the school day or working hours. Pressures and demands at work can sway who we are and how we do it into a personality that favors more online likes than the authentic interactions we need to establish deep relationships with the students we serve. So, we need grace more than ever.

Throughout this book, you'll read stories and strategies that will allow you to walk away with key practices and exercises that will build confidence so you can extend grace with others. School leader, author, and keynote speaker Jessica Cabeen provides frames that will empower anyone—teacher, principal, parent, or superintendent—to lead with grace:

- Snapshot: A story of grace in action.
- Grace defined: A description of the skill and how to strengthen abilities to lead.
- Grace in practice: Ways to grow in the soft skills in your daily interactions with others.
- Grace in action: Challenges for you to create ways to put this practice in place tomorrow.

MODERN MENTOR
Reimagining Teacher Mentorship

By Suzy Brooks (@simplysuzy) & Matthew X. Joseph (@matthewxjoseph)

As modern mentors, how can we shift our practices as individuals or make widespread change happen in our systems? Mentoring is not the process of checking a box; it is the process of developing colleagues who eventually work alongside us in a challenging profession where collaboration, connection, and consistency are all vital for our students.

If you want to know exactly what you will get, you need a menu of strategies! This book showcases ways to develop mentoring programs, designed to assist teachers in becoming strong mentors and to assist new teachers in getting the most out of their mentoring relationship.

Veteran educators, recognized school leaders, and expert mentors Suzy Brooks and Matthew X. Joseph bring you the Stories and Strategies that will help you turn novice educators into EduStars.

HACKING EDUCATION
10 Quick Fixes For Every School

By Mark Barnes (@markbarnes19) & Jennifer Gonzalez (@cultofpedagogy)

In the award-winning first Hack Learning Series book, *Hacking Education*, Mark Barnes and Jennifer Gonzalez employ decades of teaching experience and hundreds of discussions with education thought leaders to show you how to find and hone the quick fixes that every school and classroom need. Using a Hacker's mentality, they provide **one Aha moment after another** with 10 Quick Fixes For Every School—solutions to everyday problems and teaching methods that any teacher or administrator can implement immediately.

"Barnes and Gonzalez don't just solve problems; they turn teachers into hackers—a transformation that is right on time."

—Don Wettrick, Author of *Pure Genius*

HACKING PROJECT BASED LEARNING

10 Easy Steps to PBL and Inquiry in the Classroom

By Ross Cooper (@rosscoops31) and Erin Murphy (@murphysmusings5)

As questions and mysteries around PBL and inquiry continue to swirl, experienced classroom teachers and school administrators Ross Cooper and Erin Murphy have written a book that will empower those intimidated by PBL to cry, "I can do this!" while at the same time providing added value for those who are already familiar with the process. Impacting teachers and leaders around the world, *Hacking Project Based Learning* demystifies what PBL is all about with **10 hacks that construct a simple path** that educators and students can easily follow to achieve success. Forget your prior struggles with project based learning. This book makes PBL an amazing gift you can give all students tomorrow!

"Hacking Project Based Learning is a classroom essential. Its ten simple 'hacks' will guide you through the process of setting up a learning environment in which students will thrive from start to finish."

—Daniel H. Pink, New York Times
Bestselling Author of *DRIVE*

HACKING ASSESSMENT
10 Ways To Go Gradeless In a Traditional Grades School
By Starr Sackstein (@mssackstein)

In the bestselling *Hacking Assessment,* award-winning teacher and world-renowned formative assessment expert Starr Sackstein unravels one of education's oldest mysteries: how to assess learning without grades—even in a school that uses numbers, letters, GPAs, and report cards. While many educators can only muse about the possibility of a world without grades, teachers like Sackstein are **reimagining education**. In this unique, eagerly-anticipated book, Sackstein shows you exactly how to create a remarkable no-grades classroom like hers, a vibrant place where students grow, share, thrive, and become independent learners who never ask, "What's this worth?"

"The beauty of the book is that it is not an empty argument against grades—but rather filled with valuable alternatives that are practical and will help to refocus the classroom on what matters most."

—ADAM BELLOW, WHITE HOUSE
PRESIDENTIAL INNOVATION FELLOW

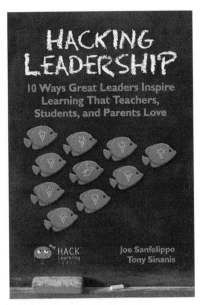

HACKING LEADERSHIP
10 Ways Great Leaders Inspire Learning That Teachers, Students, and Parents Love

By Joe Sanfelippo (@joe_sanfelippo) and Tony Sinanis (@tonysinanis)

In the runaway bestseller *Hacking Leadership*, internationally known school leaders Joe Sanfelippo and Tony Sinanis bring readers inside schools that few stakeholders have ever seen—places where students not only come first but have a unique voice in teaching and learning. Sanfelippo and Sinanis ignore the bureaucracy that stifles many leaders, focusing instead on building a culture of **engagement, transparency and, most importantly, fun**. *Hacking Leadership* has superintendents, principals, and teacher leaders around the world employing strategies they never before believed possible and learning how to lead from the middle. Want to revolutionize teaching and learning at your school or district? *Hacking Leadership* is your blueprint. Read it today, energize teachers and learners tomorrow!

"The authors do a beautiful job of helping leaders focus inward, instead of outward. This is an essential read for leaders who are, or want to lead, learner-centered schools."

—GEORGE COUROS, AUTHOR OF *THE INNOVATOR'S MINDSET*

HACKING SCHOOL CULTURE

Designing Compassionate Classrooms

By Angela Stockman
(@angelastockman) and
Ellen Feig Gray (@ellenfeiggray)

Bullying prevention and character-building programs are deepening our awareness of how today's kids struggle and how we might help, but many agree: They aren't enough to create school cultures where students and staff flourish. This inspired Angela Stockman and Ellen Feig Gray to begin seeking out systems and educators who were getting things right. Their experiences taught them that the real game changers are using a human-centered approach. Inspired by other design thinkers, many teachers are creating learning environments where seeking a greater understanding of themselves and others is the highest standard. They're also realizing that **compassion is best cultivated in the classroom,** not the boardroom or the auditorium. It's here that we learn how to pull one another close. It's here that we begin to negotiate the distances between us, too.

"*Hacking School Culture: Designing Compassionate Classrooms* is a valuable addition to the Hack Learning Series. It provides concrete support and suggestions for teachers to improve their interactions with their students at the same time they enrich their own professional experiences. Although primarily aimed at K–12 classrooms, the authors' insightful suggestions have given me, a veteran college professor, new insights into positive classroom dynamics which I have already begun to incorporate into my classes."

—LOUISE HAINLINE, PH.D., PROFESSOR OF PSYCHOLOGY,
BROOKLYN COLLEGE OF CUNY

HACKING EARLY LEARNING

10 Building Blocks to Success in Pre-K–3 That All Teachers and School Leaders Should Know

By Jessica Cabeen (@jessicacabeen)

School readiness, closing achievement gaps, partnering with families, and innovative learning are just a few of the reasons the **early learning years are the most critical** years in a child's life. In what ways have schools lost the critical components of early learning—preschool through third grade—and how can we intentionally bring those ideas and instructional strategies back? In *Hacking Early Learning*, kindergarten school leader, early childhood education specialist, and Minnesota State Principal of the Year Jessica Cabeen provides strategies for teachers, principals, and district administrators for best practices in preschool through third grade, including connecting these strategies to all grade levels.

"Jessica Cabeen is not afraid to say she's learned from her mistakes and misconceptions. But it is those mistakes and misconceptions that qualify her to write this book, with its wonderfully user-friendly format. For each problem specified, there is a hack and actionable advice presented as "What You Can Do Tomorrow" and "A Blueprint for Full Implementation." Jessica's leadership is informed by both head and heart and, because of that, her wisdom will be of value to those who wish to teach and lead in the early childhood field."

—Rae Pica, Early Childhood Education Keynote Speaker and Author of *What If Everybody Understood Child Development?*

Adam Chamberlin & Svetoslav Matejic

UNDERSTANDING APATHY,
ENGAGEMENT, AND MOTIVATION
IN THE CLASSROOM

QUIT POINT:
Understanding Apathy, Engagement, and Motivation in the Classroom
By Adam Chamberlin and Svetoslav Matejic (@pomme_ed)

Two classroom teachers grew tired of apathy in their classrooms, so they asked two simple but crucial questions: Why do students quit? And more importantly, what should we do about it? In *Quit Point: Understanding Apathy, Engagement, and Motivation in the Classroom*, authors Chamberlin and Matejic present a new way of approaching those issues. The Quit Point—their theory on how, why, and when people quit and how to stop quitting before it happens—will **transform how teachers reach the potential of each and every student.**

Quit Point reveals how to confront apathy and build student engagement; interventions to challenge students to keep going; and how to experience a happier, more fulfilling, teaching experience—starting tomorrow. Researchers, school leaders, and teachers have wondered for centuries what makes students stop working. Now, the answer is finally here. Read *Quit Point* today and stop quitting in your school or class before it begins.

HACKING ENGAGEMENT
50 Tips & Tools to Engage Teachers and Learners Daily

By James Alan Sturtevant (@jamessturtevant)

Some students hate your class. Others are just bored. Many are too nice, or too afraid, to say anything about it. Don't let it bother you; it happens to the best of us. But now, it's **time to engage!** In *Hacking Engagement*, the seventh book in the Hack Learning Series, veteran high school teacher, author, and popular podcaster James Sturtevant provides 50—that's right five-oh—tips and tools that will engage even the most reluctant learners daily. Sold in dozens of countries around the world, *Hacking Engagement* has become an educator's go-to guide for better student engagement in all grades and subjects. In fact, this book is so popular, Sturtevant penned a follow-up, *Hacking Engagement Again*, which brings 50 more powerful strategies. Find both at HackLearningBooks.com.

HACKING DIGITAL LEARNING STRATEGIES

10 Ways to Launch EdTech Missions in Your Classroom

By Shelly Sanchez Terrell (@ShellTerrell)

In this breakthrough book, international EdTech presenter and NAPW Woman of the Year Shelly Sanchez Terrell demonstrates the power of EdTech Missions—lessons and projects that inspire learners to use web tools and social media to innovate, research, collaborate, problem-solve, campaign, crowd fund, crowdsource, and publish. The 10 Missions in *Hacking DLS* are more than enough to transform how teachers integrate technology, but there's also much more here. Included in the book is a **38-page Mission Toolkit**, complete with reproducible mission cards, badges, polls, and other handouts that you can copy and distribute to students immediately.

"The secret to Shelly's success as an education collaborator on a global scale is that she shares information most revered by all educators, information that is original, relevant, and vetted, combining technology with proven education methodology in the classroom. This book provides relevance to a 21st-century educator."

—THOMAS WHITBY, AUTHOR, PODCASTER, BLOGGER, CONSULTANT, CO-FOUNDER OF #EDCHAT

HACKING CLASSROOM MANAGEMENT

10 Ideas To Help You Become the Type of Teacher They Make Movies About

By Mike Roberts (@baldroberts)

Utah English Teacher of the Year and sought-after speaker Mike Roberts brings you 10 quick and easy classroom management hacks that will **make your classroom the place to be** for all your students. He shows you how to create an amazing learning environment that actually makes discipline, rules, and consequences obsolete, no matter if you're a new teacher or a 30-year veteran teacher.

"Mike writes from experience; he's learned, sometimes the hard way, what works and what doesn't, and he shares those lessons in this fine little book. The book is loaded with specific, easy-to-apply suggestions that will help any teacher create and maintain a classroom where students treat one another with respect, and where they learn."

—CHRIS CROWE, ENGLISH PROFESSOR AT BYU, PAST PRESIDENT OF ALAN, AUTHOR OF *DEATH COMING UP THE HILL, GETTING AWAY WITH MURDER: THE TRUE STORY OF THE EMMETT TILL CASE; MISSISSIPPI TRIAL, 1955*

HACKING THE WRITING WORKSHOP
Redesign with Making in Mind

By Angela Stockman (@AngelaStockman)

Agility matters. This is what Angela Stockman learned when she left the classroom over a decade ago to begin supporting young writers and their teachers in schools. What she learned transformed her practice and led to the publication of her primer on this topic: *Make Writing: 5 Teaching Strategies that Turn Writer's Workshop Into a Maker Space.* Now, Angela is back with more stories from the road and **plenty of new thinking to share.** In *Make Writing*, Stockman upended the traditional writing workshop by combining it with the popular ideas that drive the maker space. Now, she is expanding her concepts and strategies and breaking new ground in *Hacking the Writing Workshop.*

"Good writing is good thinking. This is a book about how to think better, for yourself and with others."

—DAVE GRAY, FOUNDER OF XPLANE, AND AUTHOR OF *THE CONNECTED COMPANY*, *GAMESTORMING*, AND *LIMINAL THINKING*

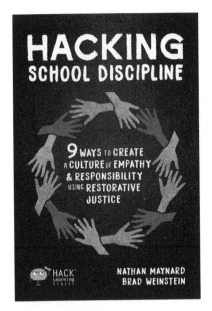

HACKING SCHOOL DISCIPLINE
9 Ways to Create a Culture of Empathy & Responsibility using Restorative Justice
By Nathan Maynard (@NmaynardEdu) and Brad Weinstein (@WeinsteinEdu)

Are you or your teachers frustrated with carrots and sticks, detention rooms, and suspension—antiquated school discipline practices that simply do not work with the students entering our classrooms today? Our kids have complex needs, and we must empower and embrace them with restorative practices that not only change behaviors but transform students into productive citizens, accountable for their own actions. In a book that should become your new blueprint for school discipline, teachers, presenters, and school leaders Nathan Maynard and Brad Weinstein demonstrate how to eliminate punishment and build a culture of responsible students and independent learners. **Before you suspend another student** ... read *Hacking School Discipline*, and build a school environment that promotes responsible learners who never need to be punished. Then watch learning soar, teachers smile, and your entire community rejoice.

RESOURCES FROM TIMES 10

SITES:

times10books.com

hacklearning.org

hacklearningbooks.com

weleadforward.com

hackingquestions.com

PODCASTS:

hacklearningpodcast.com

jamesalansturtevant.com/podcast

FREE TOOLS FOR EDUCATORS:

hacklearningtoolkit.com

leadforwardpreview.com

greatleadershipwebinar.com

ON TWITTER:

@HackMyLearning

@LeadForward2

#LeadForward

#HackLearning

#ChasingGreatness

#HackingLeadership

#HackingMath

#HackingEngagement

#HackingPBL

#MakeWriting

#EdTechMissions

#HackingEarlyLearning

#CompassionateClassrooms

#HackYourLibrary

#QuitPoint

#HackingQs

#HackingSchoolDiscipline

#LeadWithGrace

HACK LEARNING ON FACEBOOK:

facebook.com/hacklearningseries

facebook.com/groups/weleadforward

HACK LEARNING ON INSTAGRAM:

hackmylearning

X10

Vision, Experience, Action

TIMES 10 is helping all education stakeholders improve every aspect of teaching and learning. We are committed to solving big problems with simple ideas. We bring you content from experts, shared through multiple channels, including books, podcasts, and an array of social networks. Our mantra is simple: Read it today; fix it tomorrow. Stay in touch with us at Times10Books.com, at #HackLearning on Twitter, and on the Hack Learning Facebook page.

Made in the USA
Columbia, SC
09 April 2020